ARCHBISHOP CORMAC
AND THE 21ST CENTURY CHURCH

ARCHBISHOP CORMAC
AND THE 21ST CENTURY CHURCH

Nick Baty

Fount

An Imprint of HarperCollins*Publishers*

Fount is an Imprint of
HarperCollins*Religious*
part of HarperCollins*Publishers*
77–85 Fulham Palace Road, London w6 8jb
www.fireandwater.com

First published in Great Britain in 2000 by Fount

1 3 5 7 9 10 8 6 4 2

A catalogue record for this book
is available from the British Library

ISBN 0 00 628169 9

Printed and bound in Great Britain by
Creative Print and Design (Wales), Ebbw Vale

For
Norman Cresswell
a good teacher and a great friend

Contents

Wherever the Catholic sun doth shine,
There's always laughter and good red wine.
At least I've always found it so.
Benedicamus Domino!

HILAIRE BELLOC

Acknowledgements

Inestimable thanks to everyone who is mentioned in this book, as well as:

Sven-Holger Brunzendorf, Paul Burnell, Catholic Media Office, Angus Clarke, Victoria Combe, Kieron Conry, Ruth Cubbin, Robert Doyle, Ian Farrell, Kevin Flaherty, Maria Francis, Gabriel Communications, Ruth Gledhill, Jackie Gregory, Patricia Hardcastle, Dunstan Harrington, Tony Heath, Tom Horwood, John Jenkinson, Joe Kelly, Jean Lamb, James MacNamara, Peter Montgomery, Marie Parry, Nuala Parsons, Huw Powell, Georgina Rand, Ruth Rees, *The Times* library, Lynda Walker, Greg Watts, Sue Wright. Special thanks to Michael Wherly for his keen eye and patience, and to Father Brian Murphy-O'Connor for his discreet indiscretions.

Nick Baty
Manchester
March 2000

From Here to Eternity?
– a Personal View

It's not much fun being Archbishop of Westminster. Cormac Murphy-O'Connor might get to live in a large house in central London opposite a pub called The Cardinal – but proximity to an inviting hostelry is about the only perk. And he'll have to work hard for the privilege.

Being so close to the seat of temporal power there will be all sorts of civic duties, including dialogue with Parliament on many issues. He will be expected to build on the excellent relationship Cardinal Hume established with Queen Elizabeth II. And, like Her Majesty, he will be expected to attend all sorts of functions and gatherings – whether he wants to or not – simply because of who he is. If his career is anything like that of his predecessors he will be given a cardinal's hat within the next decade, probably sooner rather than later, and will be summoned to Rome to elect a Pope should a vacancy occur in the next few years.

The pundits have already labelled him 'leader of Catholics in England & Wales' – which he is not, as the Catholic Church in Britain has no equivalent position to that of the Archbishop of Canterbury. Officially his jurisdiction extends only to the boundaries of his diocese and he has already said he intends to do in Westminster 'what I have been striving to do for the past 22 years in the Diocese of Arundel & Brighton, namely, teaching and preaching the Good News of Jesus Christ and endeavouring to be a shepherd, a guide and pastor of the people'.

That is, if he is allowed to. For he will receive stiff letters from people all over the country who believe the Church is too liberal, and petitions from those who believe it is too conservative. And he'll have to be careful what he says – plenty of Britain's 'dissident' bishops have been reported directly to Rome.

Before his installation, newspapers and television reporters had already assigned him the job of stemming the exodus from the pews. And he had been labelled a 'liberal' as well as being described as a 'traditionalist'.

Archbishop Cormac is a keen rugby fan and a talented pianist but it might be useful if he can add juggling to his list of accomplishments, for he will be expected to perform all sorts of impossible tasks by all sorts of people of all sorts of persuasions. Because while the majority of Catholic parishes in England & Wales are getting on with the everyday tasks of celebrating the sacraments, educating their children and raising money to repair the organ or send a sick person to Lourdes, there are a few rocking the boat – and they're not doing it quietly. These are the 'liberals' and 'traditionalists' who claim to have all the answers and who are, doubtless, already fuming over Archbishop Cormac's refusal to stand in either corner.

He made this clear the day he was elected: 'If by a liberal, you mean someone who is open to all new things that come along, then I am not. I am a Catholic bishop who respects the tradition of the Church. If by a conservative, you mean someone who is rigid, a fundamentalist, then I am not that either. I am a man of the Church.'

The agitators standing in opposing corners will not be cheered by those words.

Having been introduced to this vale of tears in a particularly damp part of North Wales, I was privileged to grow up in the cultural, political, social and religious centre of the world – Merseyside. This was in the days when many of the parishes had a huge Irish population and the only time the parish social club closed the evening's proceedings with 'God Save the Queen' was on St Patrick's Day.

I was a pre-Vatican II baby, just. I remember little of the Tridentine liturgy although I can sing, from memory, the whole of Missa de Angelis, the Pater Noster and quite a few Benediction hymns, all learned partly from a love of music but mostly from a fear of our primary school headmistress.

My earliest memory of news was my parents' disgust at the scenes in Northern Ireland in 1967. They had seen TV coverage of a priest throwing some kind of projectile at the army and were shocked beyond belief. I also have vague memories of being taken to see the crib on Christmas afternoon and thanking Baby Jesus for my new tricycle.

I remember, too, believing that everyone in the world was Catholic – well, all my parents' friends were Catholics, as were all my friends' parents. We didn't quite live in a Catholic ghetto but we certainly lived in a self-sustaining community. If you needed anything doing, there was someone at church who had that skill, and our parish priest could have almost anything done for nothing. Even the chaps who didn't come to Mass – they used to say a good Merseyside Catholic is a man whose wife goes to church – wouldn't have dared to charge the Canon for their services.

I was the angelic-looking altar boy who, declared the old ladies of the parish, would find my reward in heaven. My mother would look on these scenes while wearing the beatific smile of a plaster saint and then remind me that I was 'a street angel and a house devil' before smacking my legs for some offence or other.

On the first Sunday of Advent 1967, my grandfather returned from the early Mass to be greeted by an enthusiastic 'What was it like, Dad?' from Mum. Grandad had been to the first 'new' Mass in our parish – the priest faced the people from behind a temporary altar table, a microphone to his left so he could be clearly heard and, most amazing, it was in English.

The effects of Vatican II would be far-reaching. But we didn't know about those then. All we knew was that, thanks to the *Novus Ordo*, we could now understand every word our priest said without the aid of a missal, although cards had been issued in the pews so we could all recite the Gloria and the Creed in English.

Then the nuns at my sister's convent school shortened their habits and a teacher at the local Catholic secondary told the girls they no longer need wear hats or mantillas for Sunday Mass. The girls' mothers followed suit and hatpins, those long skewers that Catholic ladies passed right through their heads, or so it appeared to a five-year-old, soon became collectors' items. Our parents were a tad mystified when we came home from school speaking of 'Jesus' and 'Mary' rather than 'our Lord' and 'our Lady', but took it to be something to do with the new metric system, or the Initial Training Alphabet (ITA) that made poor spellers of many of my generation.

Most of 'the changes' appeared to be on the surface and in line with Pope John XXIII's command that the windows should be thrown open to let in the fresh air. Even the worrying innovation of evangelical-style prayer groups, organized by the local Faithful Companions of Jesus, were explained as a good thing by our bishop. 'What could possibly be wrong with people praying together?' he said. Still, we weren't quite prepared for the gifts of the Holy Spirit, first made manifest at Pentecost, suddenly appearing in a formerly sedate convent in Birkenhead. Those speaking in tongues, prophesying and being slain in the Spirit were seen as, at best, a little eccentric and, at worst, three beads short of a full rosary.

But all in all, this was the Church my parents' generation had known from childhood and those of us now under 40 were scarcely old enough to notice any 'changes' at all. We fumbled along, telling our parents we'd been to Mass when we hadn't, leaving the Church, coming back, asking questions, arguing about the rules, but basically Catholics at heart. As the novelist Michael Carson once described it, this was 'Cathoholism', an addiction to our upbringing which was more than a little difficult to break.

For more than 400 years Catholics had, at least in theory, held the same beliefs the world over. There were slightly different forms of art and music from nation to nation, but on the whole Catholics were truly catholic. Then, at some point in the latter part of the 20th century, Catholics began to disagree with one another and rows broke out that are still reverberating.

'Progressives' and 'traditionalists' started to appear, both claiming to have the definitive answer. It was like watching a debate across the floor of the House of Commons, with most of us ordinary folk in the pew stuck up in the strangers' gallery, unable to voice our opinion or even to understand the argument.

Mass was now available with hard rock or classical music depending on which church you went to – but usually according to the priest's preference rather than the congregation's. Organs and choirs were banned in some churches, guitars and flutes prohibited in others. Parishioners watched in horror as a new parish priest consigned a much-loved baptismal font to the cellar, and again when his successor discovered and restored a much-loathed statue.

Theologians came out of their lecture halls and began airing their doubts in public. Religious who had given up their independent schools and private hospitals to work in the second and third worlds came back speaking of liberation theology, claiming it was as relevant for the inner cities as it was for the shanty towns of Peru – while their opponents simply declared it Marxist.

The problem facing the Church in England & Wales today isn't the empty pews and deserted seminaries. It isn't how we worship or how we interpret the documents of Vatican II. It's the disagreements and divisions among the people of God. There's a clamour from left and right, from progressive and traditionalist. And a stranger venturing into our community would have to clap his hands over his ears to find out what we really believe.

When, late in 1999, I started researching for this book I realized I'd opened something of a can of worms. I wished I could reseal the lid and pop it back on the supermarket shelf for some other unsuspecting shopper to pick up and drop into their trolley.

One day I discovered that 'we don't have enough priests' and the next that 'the Church is dominated by the clergy'. Divorced and remarried Catholics 'are made to feel non-people' while 'priests are bending the rules simply to accommodate people living in sin'. Gay Catholics are 'marginalized' but it is gay clergy who are 'keeping women in their place by defending their little boys' club'.

Apparently 'our bishops are divided' while 'hiding behind the corporate façade of the bishops' conference'. Priests 'do not support their brother priests' and 'the National Conference of priests is just another all-male ghetto'. It would appear that 'the Church is stuck in the Dark Ages' while also bending over backwards and 'pandering to modern society'.

Even Catholic women's groups disagree on which of them is getting it right, which of them is the most Catholic. Did you know that 'women don't have a voice in the Church' but have also been busy 'infiltrating the hierarchy'? (Apparently members of one group have been sneaking into the meetings of another in order to expose the latter's subterfuge.)

Both liberals and conservatives have found themselves in more than tepid water for expressing their opinions. At least two progressive nuns have had to duck warning shots from the Vatican's big guns. And one traditionalist group – which was proving something of a thorn in the mitre of every bishop in the country – was even threatened by Archbishop's House with legal action.

We're rather lucky here in Britain. We're not a persecuted or underground church or afraid of voicing our opinion. We can afford the decadence of debate while large numbers of our Christian brothers and sisters live under oppressive regimes or fight daily battles against death and disease. Our rows about the removal of altar rails or the demolition of an old church wouldn't register with them, or would baffle them completely. Theirs is a life of survival rather than a debate over liturgical niceties.

Perhaps we have too few challenges these days – or perhaps we don't see them. If we really addressed ourselves to how we can best practise our beliefs in an increasingly secular world we wouldn't have time to argue about sexual mores or to report supposedly 'dissident' bishops to Rome.

A priest friend begged me to make the point that, while all that noise is going on, it's coming from a very small minority, if a minority can be so qualified. 'The majority of people are just trying to get on with their lives as best they can,' he says. I suspect he's right and would like to count myself among them.

Perhaps there is a split in the Church these days. But I don't believe it's between the 'progressives' and the 'traditionalists'. Like the Labour and Tory parties, they are beginning to sing from the same hymnsheet – and that hymnsheet has been produced by the Babel Printing Co. Ltd. The split is between those people who try to live the Christian life and those who argue about the best way to do it. Archbishop Cormac has an almost impossible task ahead of him.

Cardinal Hume had to cope with traditionalists who feared the Church in England & Wales was straying too far from Roman dictates, as well as liberals who thought it was being manipulated by the Vatican. Both groups hope Archbishop Cormac's time in office will redress the balance.

In the red corner is We Are Church UK, part of an international group lobbying for change on 'the big problems', including women's ordination and the recognition of gay relationships. 'There's no proper dialogue,' says co-ordinator Valerie Stroud. 'The bishops are being used as the doers of Rome's will. Archbishop Cormac is good for our time and I would hope he'd be prepared to listen to ordinary people in the Church and engage over the big problems. The only way we're going to solve them is by all members of the society that is the Church talking about them and finding a common way forward. But the bishops are frightened of setting foot outside the strictures that Rome places upon them.'

Far from it, counters the traditionalist group Pro Ecclesia et Pontifice (for the Church and the Pope, or PEEP for short), which claims the hierarchy are doing many things they oughtn't and which encourages members to report those 'dissident' bishops to the Vatican. PEEP chairman Daphne McLeod has been so vociferous in her opposition to the religious education schemes approved by the bishops that on one occasion there were attempts to silence her. But Mrs McLeod remains undaunted and says it is her duty to fight on.

Cardinal Hume was publicly praised and pilloried both for adhering to traditional Catholic teaching and for appearing to stray from it. Within days of his appointment being announced, Archbishop Cormac had already received vitriolic letters telling him what was wrong with the Church and what he has to do to put it right. On the other hand, he has also received dozens of bars of dark chocolate since his brother, Father Brian Murphy-O'Connor, revealed the new archbishop's particular vice.

The archbishop has been accused of being too liberal, to which he replied, 'If I am a liberal then the Pope is a liberal.' The fact that he has, for many years, been entrusted with the job of working on ecumenical matters on behalf of the bishops of England & Wales, has been taken to mean that he is in favour of somehow protestantizing Catholicism. Not so, he said the day before his installation: 'I utterly deny that it is somehow equal to watering down the Catholic faith. On the contrary, I do not think you can be a proper Catholic without being an ecumenicist. My ecumenical work has made me more convinced of my Catholicity.'

Friends say Archbishop Cormac is the ideal man to handle the rows and the disputes, however acrimonious. He is able to remain calm and coherent in the most furious debates. Throughout his career he has sought to build up a family atmosphere in the Church – and that word 'family' pops up with almost annoying regularity over the next few chapters.

In his 1984 book *The Family of the Church*, Archbishop Cormac writes: 'Indeed Catholics have especially discovered since the Vatican Council, the problems of internal dialogue within a single denomination are almost as acute as dialogue with other denominations.'

He is right. Catholics with an agenda can be far more unpleasant to each other than they are to Christians of other churches. Just take a look at some of the letters pages in the weekly Catholic newspapers. While there are many contributions about matters of social justice and evangelization or simply letters from people spreading the good news about local events, there are far too many from extremist groups arguing about which one of them is getting things right. Letters published in the Catholic press four days after Archbishop Cormac's installation argued – and not in the most Christian fashion – about the siting of church fixtures and fittings, the state of church music and why Pope John Paul should not have apologized for all the wrong done in the Church's name over the last 2,000 years.

While Archbishop Cormac has spent years working to bring the Christian churches together, splinter groups have been trying to tear his own church apart. He encouraged his diocese of Arundel & Brighton to talk to each other as a family, and he can only hope that model may now be adopted by the rest of the country. Or must Archbishop Cormac, like his predecessor, be constantly harangued by those with their own, out-of-tune, drums to bang?

Perhaps it's more than a coincidence that Archbishop's House is opposite such an appealing pub!

✝

1. The Wandering Minstrel

On 22 March 2000, the bishops of England & Wales gathered in Westminster Cathedral for the first time since the death of Cardinal Basil Hume. Exactly 150 years after Pope Pius IX had restored the hierarchy, the successors of 19th-century bishops like Wiseman, Ullathorne, Brown, Briggs and Hendren gathered to witness the installation of Cormac Murphy-O'Connor as the tenth Archbishop of Westminster. As the magnificent procession made its way down the aisle of architect John Bentley's neo-Byzantine church, it was difficult to imagine that, 50 years before, the tall, majestically vested figure at the rear was adorned in Japanese robes and taking his curtain calls following a performance of Gilbert & Sullivan's *The Mikado*.

Cormac Murphy-O'Connor might now be the most prominent among the leaders of Catholics in England & Wales but in the 1950s, as a young student at the English College, Rome, he brought the house down with his interpretation of wandering minstrel Nanki-Poo, only son of the Emperor of Japan. The Mikado was played with great aplomb by Archbishop Michael Bowen of Southwark, and Katisha, his daughter-in-law elect, by a young man with flaming red hair, now better known as Bishop John Brewer of Lancaster. Many other respected and respectable monsignors and canons appeared in that production as the Gentlemen of Japan and the chorus of Japanese Ladies, in itself a feat of costume design.

'We were fresh-faced youths but it's amazing what you can do,' recalls make-up artist Richard Incledon, now a septuagenarian canon of Arundel & Brighton Cathedral Chapter. 'Cormac was always a man. He was too tall and bony-faced so he wasn't a suitable case for treatment for the girls' chorus. But he has a very natural, attractive singing voice.' Indeed, at 6ft 4in, Archbishop Cormac is slightly taller than Cardinal Basil Hume and he is slightly broader too. As one of the Westminster Cathedral clergy has already commented, 'he shows off the vestments very well'.

When they began their studies in the autumn of 1950, those 'Gentlemen of Japan' believed they could change the world. It was a time of confidence for the Church and there was hope of a new golden age for British Catholicism. The Church in England & Wales was celebrating the centenary of its formal re-establishment and the restoration of the system of diocesan bishops. Churches bombed during the war had been rebuilt and the advent of new towns meant many new churches were under construction. With the full implementation of the 1944 Education Act there was a secondary school building boom too. The Catholic Church wasn't just blossoming, it was exploding.

'In some ways our generation was particularly fortunate,' says Canon Incledon. 'There was a great surge of confidence in the Church after the war. There were Christian democratic parties in France, Germany and Italy. The Church was coming back out of its corner into the public world.

'We were all set to convert England within a generation and see the whole thing back in the fold. We had an attitude of absolute confidence and optimism which, on reflection, was possibly about the wrong things, but that attitude of confidence has remained.

'We were old enough to have inherited that habit of basic confidence but young enough to ride the punches with the change. People older than us found change harder. We found it easier but somehow kept something of those old attitudes. A feeling that we were in the right ship.'

Fifty years on, those 'fresh-faced youths' are still good friends. They meet together every five years and it is often music and entertainment that reunites them, with Archbishop Cormac pounding away at the piano, performing everything from Mozart, through jazz, to the traditional Irish melodies that he learned from his parents. Presumably his fellow priests will still remember the words if he breaks into a chorus of 'Three Little Maids from School'.

Even the most oak-like of archbishops must start life as a little acorn, and Cormac Murphy-O'Connor was planted in a forest of priests and religious on 24 August 1932. There were already three priest uncles in the family; two of Cormac's older brothers, Patrick and John, and three first cousins – including the renowned scholar Father Jerome Murphy O'Connor – would also be ordained. Priests were in and out of the Murphy-O'Connor household and his GP father, Patrick George Murphy-O'Connor, had enough influence with the Presentation Brothers in Ireland to persuade them to come to Reading to open a new school. So the young Cormac's interest in pursuing a career in the Church was not seen as at all unusual.

As a child Cormac was asked what he would like to be when he grew up. 'Doctor or Pope,' he replied. He achieved the first title through academic study but has recently been reported as saying that 'anybody who wanted to be Pope would need to have his head tested'.

The Murphy-O'Connors hailed from County Cork where Cormac's grandfather was a vintner. The family were business people at least as far back as the early 19th century, and the hyphenated surname could be described as a business deal in itself. Cork's business community was dominated by four families: the McSweeneys, the Murphys, the O'Connors and the Sheehans. Nearly 200 years ago, a Miss McSweeney married a Mr Murphy and, following her husband's death, went on to marry an O'Connor. Presumably such marriages increased business opportunities all round, and so the widow Murphy became Mrs Murphy-O'Connor. She had two sons by her first marriage who went on to become priests. One of them, Father Denis Murphy, became parish priest of Kinsale and his brother, Daniel, was consecrated the first Bishop of Hyderabad in India. Even this far back, before the Great Famine, there were priests called McSweeney who were nephews of that first Mrs Murphy-O'Connor. All in all, Cormac's early desire to be a priest could be said to be following very much in the family business.

'I knew from the age of six that I wanted to be a priest,' says his older brother, Father Brian, 'and I think Cormac was the same, although my parents wouldn't do anything to encourage us, they didn't want us to be forced in any way. When I asked them, at the age of 14, they said I should wait a couple of years and make another decision, which I did. But there was never any pressure put on us.'

Father Brian is just an inch shorter than his younger brother – eldest brother Jim, a retired doctor, is the tallest at 6ft 6in – and there is a striking physical resemblance. Even their voices are disconcertingly similar. In fact, Father Brian could easily stand in for his brother, should the new archbishop be called to Rome during a particularly hectic time.

Archbishop Cormac's parents first emigrated to Liverpool. His doctor father, Patrick, worked there as a locum before buying a house and practice in Reading, where all six children were born. The Murphy-O'Connors were devoted Catholics, daily Mass-goers who were equally dedicated to the social life and work of the parish. Patrick was the founder and president of the St Vincent de Paul Society in Reading and received a papal knighthood in recognition of his work, although even his six children knew little at the time of how much he did. Father Brian explains that 'I only found out in later years how good my father was, looking after the poor and downtrodden in Reading.'

Their mother, Ellen, founded the Union of Catholic Mothers in the town and was a school governor. 'She was a great lady,' says Father Brian. 'She was tall, commanding, a very good person. But to us, of course, she was just "Mum".' In fact Ellen was 'Mum' six times over. Ten years after Cormac, the youngest of her five sons, was born she gave birth to a daughter, Catherine.

In his 1984 book *The Family of the Church*, Archbishop Cormac described his family background as 'a very Catholic one':

We used to have family prayers every evening and nothing was ever allowed to interrupt that. I think the only things my father cared about were his family and the Church. Even his profession – he was a family doctor – was an expression and completion of his faith.

Pope Paul once described the family as the *ecclesiola*, the little church, and I suppose that was particularly true in my case because it was from my own family that I received so much of my understanding of the Church. It was there in my family life, like so many others in similar families, that I learnt the meaning and the value of prayer, of worship, of forgiveness and of love.

Of course, my understanding of the Church in its wider context has broadened and deepened since those early years, but the connection of family and Church is a very real one.

Not that the Murphy-O'Connor household should be perceived as living in perpetual piety. This was a family that played together as much as it prayed together.

'We were mad card players,' says Father Brian. 'One particular Irish game we played incessantly was A Hundred and Ten. It's one we understood because we were reared with it, but no one else does. We used to get anyone coming to visit us to play A Hundred and Ten so we could beat them. In fact, when I was seven I gave up playing cards for Lent and the whole family had to give up as well because I was so miserable.

'And we were all brilliant sportsmen. You must put that in as well,' he laughs. 'My eldest brother Jim played for Ireland, Father Pat played for Gosport, my brother John played for the Artillery, I played for the Isle of Wight and Cormac played for Portsmouth. On one occasion Jim, Pat, John, Brian and I all played for Gosport. Cormac couldn't play that day as he was playing for the Vatican.'

Obviously as good at rugby as he was at the family's dubious-sounding card game, Cormac also excelled at music. 'We were all offered the chance to be taught how to play the piano,' says

Father Brian. 'But Cormac was the only one who stuck to it. Father Pat played the guitar but that was only twanging chords.'

Young Cormac's love of music and sport was further encouraged when, after attending Presentation College, Reading, he followed his four older brothers to Prior Park College, Bath. Douglas Lascelles first met Cormac one Thursday evening when, as a rather nervous student teacher, he was feeling lost as he made his way up the hill in the dark to the sixth-form block. 'A tall young man with a fine imposing voice' leaned over the banisters and asked 'Are you taking us tonight, Sir?' 'And that was himself,' says Mr Lascelles. 'Although I must admit that what impressed me most about Cormac was that his brother played rugby for Ireland.'

Piano teacher Miss Norah Hodges considered Cormac her star pupil. But Latin master Sidney Ash recalls the youngster as 'the only pupil, that I can remember, that I ever found sound asleep in one of my classes'. It's tempting to think that Mr Ash has a selective memory on the fascination of Latin lessons, but he speaks fondly of his old pupil, whom he describes as 'a darling man'.

'Cormac and a few pals skipped out one night to go for a midnight bathe in the river,' explains Mr Ash. 'The housemaster realized that they were missing and was waiting to catch them when they came back. He said that, as they obviously didn't value their beds very much, they could spend the night sitting up at a study desk which was far from comfortable and not conducive to sleep. So when it came to classes in the morning Cormac was ready to have a nap and that's just what he did.'

At the age of 18 Cormac had the talent and technical ability to pursue a career in either music or sport. But his childhood ambition to become a priest had not faded and so, in the autumn of 1950, he began his studies at the Venerable English College, Rome.

Two of Cormac's elder brothers, Patrick and Brian, were already students at the English College and so, for one year, the three brothers were all in Rome together. 'It was most unusual to have three brothers in the college at the same time,' recalls Monsignor

Michael Buckley, who was then in his final year. 'None of them was a loner and they all made their mark, especially Pat who was the best known and most loved student in Rome. Pat took part in everything, even playing in the same football team as Karol Wojtyla [later Pope John Paul II] who was then a student at the Polish College. In later years, when it was announced in the Vatican that a Murphy-O'Connor had been appointed a bishop, everyone thought it was Pat. I'd always told Cormac his chances of an episcopacy were impossible with the three names he had. Cormac is very Irish and Murphy-O'Connor is Irish *and* double barrelled.'

While Cormac might have been nursemaided by his older siblings, he proved to be an independent type, able to make friends easily, and rather better at handling cash than his brothers. 'Pat and I used to try and get money out of him when we were bust,' recalls Father Brian.

One St Patrick's Day, this trinity of Murphy-O'Connors flirted with danger by sneaking out the back door of the college to attend a party given by the Irish Augustinians, against the rector's express instructions. 'We had a very good party,' says Father Brian. 'Then when we came back in, there was the rector standing just inside the door. He said, "I hope you had a nice time, lads."'

The young Cormac is remembered by contemporaries at the English College as a student who worked hard to achieve the best results he could. 'He systematically worked with less than ten talents and made them profitable,' one of them recalls. It's tempting to think this elderly priest's memory is unreliable, as Cormac managed to attain degrees in both philosophy and theology from the Gregorian University while also pursuing his love of sport. He played football and cricket and excelled at table tennis, but his real forte was rugby, in which he had developed such good technical skills that he was soon invited to play professionally for CUS Roma.

'He said he couldn't accept because he was in a seminary,' recalls fellow rugby player Monsignor Jack Kennedy, now a parish priest in Southport. 'They offered him everything – they even offered to buy him a chalice when he was ordained. But eventually they asked him to play one game, which he did, and we all went to watch him. He played in the centre, he was quite fast and had a good pair of hands.'

Apart from this moment of sporting glory, Cormac also played in the English College team, sometimes captained by older brother Brian, and augmented by students from New Zealand and novice Holy Ghost Fathers to make up the Vatican XV. 'We had a very, very strong side,' says Monsignor Kennedy. 'Rugby was then in its infancy in Italy and we once played the Italian national team, who wanted to practise. We played them and they beat us 12–0. The Italians are now playing in the Six Nations.'

Following his ordination in October 1956, Father Cormac was appointed curate at Corpus Christi parish, North End, Portsmouth. Assistant priests were still called curates in those days and could expect to learn the hard way – by doing what the parish priest told them, or what he allowed them to do. But Father Cormac is remembered for the youthful zest with which he organized the parish youth club, launched the parish magazine and arranged parish pilgrimages to Lourdes.

He threw himself into the round of parish visiting and, having travelled everywhere by bike, knows every street in the district to this day. More than 40 years later, he still remembers whole families and always stops to chat to his old parishioners wherever he meets them, never, it is said, forgetting a name.

'Father Cormac used to sing at the drop of a hat,' remembers parishioner Kathleen Coughlin. 'He used to sing all those great Italian arias and all the old Irish songs – he has a great singing voice. He visited people's houses, that was the great thing about him, and that's why he knows so many people. We were his first parish, of course, and I suppose everybody remembers something of their first job, but he's interested in people. He's a real people's man and he's equally at home with young people, old people, anybody. He's at home with ordinary people and yet he can take his place with the highest in the land.'

Mrs Coughlin is one of the many Corpus Christi parishioners who, for the last 20 years, have annually visited their old curate at Bishop's House in Storrington. 'There's quite a gang of us that still know him and he's kept in touch with us. He always entertains us, plays the piano for us, and we have a real sing-song. He has all the nuns baking buns and making tea for us and he comes in wheeling the trolley with his lovely dog.'

Father Cormac's second appointment was to Sacred Heart parish, Fareham, in 1963. His sporting days were far from over and he played fly-half for Portsmouth Rugby Club. But again it was Father Cormac's love of music and of people of all ages that endeared him to parishioners. Peggy McGovern remembers the young priest sitting her daughter on his knee and teaching her to sing 'Molly Malone', a song that he would rattle off at many social gatherings.

'He was a wonderful man and a wonderful priest,' says Mrs McGovern. 'He was always jolly. He took my son and a gang of the boys off to Bournemouth on retreat. I think he hoped my son might become a priest – which he didn't – but all the young ones loved him. He got on wonderfully well with everyone but more so with the young people. He left a great impression on them, as he did on all of us. You couldn't criticize him – it would be impossible to criticize him, he was such a wonderful priest. There have been some really wonderful priests here but none of them has left the same impression as Father Murphy-O'Connor.'

Christina Greenfield remembers Father Cormac and his brother Patrick cycling the four miles from Fareham to Our Lady of Walsingham, the chapel-of-ease serving parishioners living in the Porchester district. 'They cycled over in all weathers and we loved both of them,' says Mrs Greenfield, who, now aged 83, is still serving as sacristan. 'Father Cormac said the first Midnight Mass in the chapel. It was only just finished and we had to walk over the builders' planks to get in. He taught the catechism to all the children in the parish and he used to take them to the seaside at Hayling Island. He's a really good man.'

Pauline Skinner and Madeline Jeffery were two of the children from Sacred Heart whom Father Cormac used to take on those swimming parties. Years later, they say, he still remembers so many of them by name.

'It never ceases to amaze me that both Father Cormac and his brother, Father Patrick, had the ability to remember not only faces but names from the past and over the years,' says Pauline. 'Whenever we met either of them, they always took time to ask about the family. The death of Patrick was a sad loss to the Catholic community.

'The last occasion I saw Bishop Cormac was in June 1998. As a treat for my birthday, my husband had taken me to dinner at the Thakeham Hotel, near Storrington, and to my surprise Bishop Cormac was also there with his party. He again remembered me and took the time to chat, ask about my family, in particular my mother, and we cheerily reminisced. He is very special to us.'

Six months after Father Cormac had performed Charles and Bernice Dartmouth's wedding ceremony – standing on a chair to sing his now famous party piece of 'Molly Malone' at the reception – he persuaded the young couple to take over the running of the parish youth club. He wasn't the sort of man you could turn down and more than one person has commented on his persuasive charm. In fact it is said that all the Murphy-O'Connors have charm.

He had taught Mrs Dartmouth catechism many years earlier. 'He told the most amazing tales,' she remembers. 'You went along for catechism but you ended up with ghost stories from Ireland. And he converted my husband Charles – I tell you that man could convert Karl Marx.'

Father Cormac even persuaded Charles Dartmouth's brother, an amateur boxer, to act as doorman at the youth club. 'I was often ably assisted by Father Cormac,' recalls Michael Dartmouth, 'although he never stayed on my station too long. We had many, many good times and although I was not a Catholic, I cannot explain why I never converted, as I was so fond of him. We've all watched his progress and we were delighted by his promotion. It couldn't happen to a nicer man.'

In 1966 Father Cormac was appointed private secretary to Bishop Worlock of Portsmouth. Worlock, later to become Archbishop of Liverpool, had been present for most of the Second Vatican Council and was pushing hard to implement its findings, particularly those concerning the laity, in his diocese. Parish Councils were to become the norm and Portsmouth was the first diocese to set up a pastoral centre specifically for the training of lay people.

Working closely with Bishop Worlock, Father Cormac is credited with much of the initial work of setting up Park Place Pastoral Centre, Fareham, which was particularly successful in its early days. However, that work included selecting and buying domestic items, which proved not to be one of his strengths. In this context he is best remembered for his poor choice of bed linen.

'Dear Cormac was in charge of setting it all up, but he was not into this sort of domesticity, it was just not his scene,' recalls one priest of Portsmouth diocese. 'It was Cormac who was responsible for choosing the nylon sheets. We cursed him for years afterwards – everybody fell out of bed because they were so slippery. And, because they were nylon, they never wore out.'

Father Cormac was also vocations promoter for Portsmouth at the time. He proved much better at encouraging young men to consider priesthood as a way of life than he was at choosing bed linen.

'He was a very good vocations director,' recalls Canon Nicholas France, who was then a senior student approaching ordination. 'He used to run vocations camps in the summer, and he certainly encouraged vocations by being a very good role model.'

It was during his time as Bishop Worlock's secretary that Father Cormac was asked to help steer the first ever National Conference of Priests. The Conference grew out of the controversies of the first Synod of European bishops in 1968. The English representative to the Synod, Monsignor Michael Buckley, had returned home, disillusioned because so many of the questions that priests in England & Wales were asking had not been addressed. Instead Cardinal Heenan invited Monsignor Buckley to organize a conference for the clergy at home. But some of the bishops were unhappy to discover that their priests were asking to debate questions of celibacy and – with *Humanae Vitae* still a topic for lively discussion – contraception. So the cardinal asked Monsignor Buckley to choose four assistants who would be seen by the bishops as having their heads firmly screwed on.

One of those four was Father Cormac, who, says Monsignor Buckley, was 'the obvious man for me'. The first conference went ahead at Wood Hall Pastoral Centre, Wetherby, in May 1970.

'We were astonished at the anger of the priests when the conference started,' says Monsignor Buckley. 'But Cormac wanted them to express their feelings without rancour and to feel that they were being listened to. His input was very good and it was through that conference that he caught the eye of Cardinal Heenan because he was able to wed the old and the new. But he was also very much a Roman man and he knew how Rome would take it. Because of his work with Bishop Worlock he knew how the bishops would take it too. Not that his heart was in the middle of the road – it was where it had to be.

'Cormac is a very intelligent man. He's not a politician, he is pastoral. He would never strike you as somebody who was a power man. He had ideas and when they weren't taken up by the clergy he went ahead and put forward another idea. But never forced his ideas down anybody's throat.'

In 1970 Father Cormac was back on the beat as parish priest of Immaculate Conception, Portswood, Southampton. But his time there was short lived. The following year, he was appointed Rector of the English College, Rome, where he had begun his own studies 20 years earlier. Yet it is possible that parishioners at Portswood didn't suffer too much upheaval, for Father Cormac's replacement was his elder brother, Father Patrick Murphy-O'Connor.

Life was less certain for ecclesiastical students in the 1970s. While Father Cormac and his contemporaries had been sure of their goal – in short, the conversion of England to Catholicism – the 60 students now entrusted to his care were far more questioning. The Second Vatican Council had not long ended and its documents were still being published and translated. There had been much dissent about teaching such as *Humanae Vitae*, the document that reiterated the traditional Church line on contraception. Some Catholics – and not a few priests and religious – were voting with their feet.

The secular world had changed drastically. The winds of change and freedom were rising and the hallowed walls of the Venerable English College were no more immune to their draughts than any other institution. 'Cormac inherited a dissident group of student priests who were adapting very poorly to the change,' recalls one of his contemporaries. 'What he brought to the English College was normality and a discipline that he explained to, but expected from, the students.' Cardinal Heenan had visited the college more than once to calm the situation and there had even been talk of closing down this 16th-century foundation, which was suffering falling numbers and, as a result, a shortage of cash.

'I think Cormac actually saved the English College,' says Father Michael Morton, a student there until his ordination in 1975. 'Cormac took very strong decisions although he was very affable. His knockabout good humour brought the students together and he got on with all kinds of people. He got on with the Vatican, he got on with the Italians and he got on with the bishops.'

During his years as Rector, Monsignor Cormac – as he had now become – encouraged students to spend more of their time in Rome's universities, instead of skulking around the college buildings, and revived several ancient customs, including an annual walk around the major towns in the hills surrounding Rome. The practice, dating back to the days of Cardinal Nicholas Wiseman, had waned – possibly because it involved the students stopping in each town for a glass of the local wine. Unless monitored, few of them would manage the full distance.

There's no doubt that Monsignor Cormac loved outings, but on one occasion he unwittingly led his students into a whole day of imbibing for which they paid heavily the following morning.

The English College employed several domestic staff from the village of Pugliano, near Naples. When these young women were due to be confirmed, the college's former Vice-Rector, John Brewer, then the newly ordained auxiliary Bishop of Shrewsbury, returned to administer the sacrament to his old staff. Together he and Monsignor Cormac, wearing their ecclesiastical purple, led a coachload of students from the college to Pugliano, and as they entered the village they were greeted with fireworks and shouts of welcome. Inside the church the altar was adorned with the finest lace, and banners hung from every statue proclaiming, 'Viva Mgr Brewer. Viva Mgr Cormac. Viva English College.'

Following the ceremony Monsignor Cormac, Bishop Brewer and the students were taken into the village hall for a meal of pasta and wine. All had their fill, quite unaware that this was only the beginning. They were then led through Pugliano from house to house, being fed and watered at each station until, after six or seven courses of food and wine, they could only just stumble back on to their coach. But this was far from the end.

They headed towards the local bishop's palace to make a courtesy call. The final part of the trek was too steep and rocky for the coach so, still wearing their purple cassocks and having had their fill of Italian hospitality, the two clerics wearily led their students up the hill as the bells rang out to welcome them. Here they were greeted as old friends – and treated to a banquet fit for a couple of bishops and a college rector. One of the men who were there recalls that 'we were well and truly oiled'. The effects of such unintentional gluttony were evident at breakfast the next morning.

But for Monsignor Cormac, such festive occasions helped build up the college's family atmosphere. When, one depressing November evening, one of the students suggested throwing a party, Monsignor Cormac readily agreed before asking, 'What reason shall we have for it?' And each year, he encouraged and cajoled students to join him for two weeks' holiday at the beginning of the summer in the college's villa on the shores of Lake Albano before they departed for England. Here they could row out into the middle of the lake and, overlooked only by the Pope's summer residence at Castel Gandalfo, enjoy picnics with wine or, as one former student put it, 'do all the things you really shouldn't do in the middle of a lake'.

Visitors to Rome were often invited to the college as guests. In 1974 one such visitor was Poland's Cardinal Karol Wojtyla, later to become Pope John Paul II. On another occasion Harold Macmillan came for lunch. The former Prime Minister cried quite openly when he spoke of friends, the same age as his dining companions, who had died during the First World War. And when the writer Iris Murdoch was living in Rome she too experienced Monsignor Cormac's hospitality at the English College. Unfortunately the Rector became rather muddled, referring to his guest throughout the meal as Edna – Edna O'Brien, that is.

'He encouraged students to enjoy Rome and to learn,' says Father Tony Churchill, who was then pursuing post-ordination studies in moral theology. 'He gave people space to grow and if people really didn't respond they had to go in the end. But he allowed relatively young men a chance to make mistakes, and gave them space. I think a lot of people grew as a result of that.'

Father Paul Hardy recalls that when, one Christmas holiday, three students couldn't afford to go away anywhere, Monsignor Cormac lent them his own car to go off into the hills for a few days. Even so, the college Rector was no soft touch.

'I well remember the day he got fed up with nobody being up in time for Morning Prayer and he went round all the culprits, including myself, knocking us up and telling us to see him during the day,' says Father Hardy. 'I left it until very late in the evening by which time he was totally fed up with everyone knocking on his door, so it rather rebounded on him. But there are not many college rectors you could do that to and not many who react in a kindly way having been tormented all day. He always knew exactly what was going on and he gently guided us. But there was a warmth in the atmosphere he created.'

Always at the forefront of ecumenical initiatives, Monsignor Cormac introduced an exchange scheme that involved students from the Anglican colleges in England coming to Rome and students from the English College going home to visit Anglican institutions. In 1977 it was Monsignor Cormac who hosted the historic visit of the Archbishop of Canterbury, Dr Donald Coggan, to Pope Paul VI. The meeting echoed a similar visit by Dr Coggan's predecessor, Dr Michael Ramsey, 11 years earlier. It was the foundation of much Anglican-Roman Catholic dialogue to come, and the future Bishop Cormac Murphy-O'Connor would be at the helm.

In the meantime Monsignor Cormac was guiding his students, entertaining distinguished guests and generally enjoying the life Rome had to offer, apart from one thing – the tea. The news soon spread back to his home diocese of Portsmouth that the Rector of the Venerable English College was missing his daily cuppa. So when a coachload of his old parishioners from Fareham went to Rome on pilgrimage they each took him a packet. It was some time before Monsignor Cormac was again short of a good old English – or should that be Irish? – cup of tea.

When, in December 1977, Cormac Murphy-O'Connor was ordained the third Bishop of Arundel & Brighton, he took as his motto the words *Gaudium et Spes* (Joy and Hope), words that, he said, expressed the 'two gifts most needed by people today'. He also vowed that he would 'always look on the Church as a family'. From a brief glance at some of the photographs in his diocesan 'family' album over the years, the 'joy and hope' are evident. Here he is at those more formal 'family' occasions, like ordinations; on numerous 'family' outings like the annual diocesan pilgrimage to Lourdes; or jumping up and down on a bouncy castle in his garden at Storrington during his annual fiesta for those members of his 'family' with disabilities. On every snap there is his huge fatherly smile and a touch of that famous Murphy-O'Connor charm.

In his first pastoral letter to the people of Arundel & Brighton diocese, Bishop Cormac said it was important to realize that 'we are family':

> Whether we are talking about parishes, schools or societies, we must start by looking at ourselves primarily

as people, as a community, as a family. We need to experience a deep sense of belonging to the Church. The local community needs to be somewhere where everyone feels at home. We need to welcome everyone more, to make people feel that the parish and liturgy are theirs for the sharing.

Those people who have known and worked with Bishop Cormac during his time in Arundel & Brighton speak of the family atmosphere he created in the diocese. Karen Goldsmith has worked closely with the Bishop since she was diocesan youth officer in the 1980s. She is now Social Concerns Co-ordinator – a post that Bishop Cormac set up – and responsible for justice and peace issues and their implementation in the parishes.

'Bishop Cormac's been very supportive of everything we've done,' she says. 'He takes a great interest.' Ms Goldsmith speaks of Bishop Cormac's family approach – there's that word cropping up yet again. She recalls the Bishop turning up with his bike for sponsored cycle rides and says that he became very involved in youth days and youth camps, playing games with the youngsters during the day but usually staying around until late at night to hear confessions or simply to spend more time with the younger members of his flock.

'He would always muck in. He has a great gift for accompaniment, for accompanying people, just taking them where they are. He was always very approachable. The kids loved him, because he was so easy to talk to. He took them as he found them, but he always pointed the way.'

Similarly, on diocesan pilgrimages to Lourdes, which are demanding at the best of times, Archbishop Cormac would spend as much time as possible with the young helpers – Arundel & Brighton takes up to 300 youngsters to the French Marian shrine every year – as well as ministering to the many sick pilgrims and leading the exhausting liturgical timetable that a trip to Lourdes entails.

'He's a very big man but there's no sense of pomp or power,' says Ms Goldsmith. 'He's a very humble, modest man but he's a

good leader. He's not afraid to lead, but he does it with great optimism and charisma. He never drives people, he never pushes
them beyond the point at which they can't cope. He always leaves
the door open and listens well, he listens carefully and is
respectful of people. He has lots of ideas and a really strong
vision, very Gospel rooted but very strong. He listens, he
consults well and he's not afraid to move forward.'

Never one to stand on ceremony, Archbishop Cormac has
often been known to abandon prepared speeches and speak
directly in response to what is going on around him. At one
school prize night he put down his text and spoke off the cuff
to the assembled parents, pupils and teachers. As one observer
recalls, 'It came across as straight from the heart, and that felt
wonderful because of the way it touched the audience.'

At another, more stuffy, engagement he was overheard whis-
pering to a neighbour, 'Oh, Peter, why do things have to clash?
It's the final day of the British Open. Who do you reckon is going
to win?'

'He has a twinkle in his eye and he's got a very keen sense
of humour and a nice lightness of touch,' says David Cleworth,
head of the Arundel & Brighton Secondary Heads Association.
'He is a man from a big Catholic family which obviously has
been used to having fun together and he likes to have fun
with people. When he comes into a room he lightens the
atmosphere. But he's also a man of great reverence, a man
who really does come across as incredibly sincere. When some
years ago we decided to have an annual residential conference,
that started off with him providing us with Mass in his own
private chapel at St Joseph's Hall in Storrington. I will always
remember that very moving time of just the 11 headteachers
with him. He's very thoughtful, very prayerful and very
sincere.'

Mr Cleworth also describes Bishop Cormac as 'a great del-
egator'. 'One could say that delegation is passing the buck, but
if Cormac delegates anything he will empower. You always feel
that once something's handed over to someone the empower-
ment goes with it. I think he realizes that if he was to take on

everything himself he would have caved in years ago. That's his saving grace, to delegate but yet empower.'

In 1990 Arundel & Brighton became the first, and so far the only, diocese in England & Wales to use the Renew programme that had been successful in several Scottish dioceses. Adapted from an American model, Renew was an all-embracing diocesan programme mostly of spiritual renewal, but with educational overtones that flowed into the liturgy. Nearly half the diocese's Mass-going Catholics became involved in the groundwork for the programme.

'A lot of people became enthusiastic about it and it drew in a lot of people who had not been involved before,' says Canon Peter Humfrey, who was then the Bishop's Vicar for Religious Education. 'Renew really got people doing things in their own community which they carried on doing afterwards. People got moved on and they didn't go back, they didn't revert.'

Renew led to 'the Diocesan Vision' and six years of intensive activity leading up to the millennium. Then, on the first Sunday of Advent 1998, Bishop Cormac announced that preparations would begin for a diocesan synod in 2002:

> We, the people of God in Surrey and Sussex, need a renewed sense of direction as the Church confronts new challenges about its identity and mission. Through this process we will decide the shape of the Church to come. We will respond to the opportunities and serious challenges we face. We will deepen and strengthen our work of evangelization – as we bring the Gospel to the people of our own time and place.

Work began in earnest around the diocese but, after just over 12 months, the scheme had to be put on hold. A diocesan synod revolves around the bishop, and in February 2000 the people of Arundel & Brighton discovered that their leader of more than 20 years was leaving to become the tenth Archbishop of Westminster.

During his time in Arundel & Brighton, Bishop Cormac sought to build good relationships with the other Christian churches. 'He has been a good person to work with,' says Eric Kemp, Anglican Bishop of Chichester. 'He did a great deal in some quite difficult situations. It was Bishop Cormac who originated the plan of the Sussex Church leaders paying visits, as a body, to various parts of Sussex and spending a whole day there as a demonstration of the fact that the churches did work together today.' Bishop Cormac compared these days to St Paul's epistles, saying they were sending themselves instead of a letter.

Bishop Cormac is an ecumenist rather than an ecumaniac. He believes that ecumenism is simply a question of the denominations listening to each other, praying together and working together. He believes unity will come in time and has often described ecumenism as 'like a road with no exit'. He says that Christian unity is the 'restoration' of one Church that in many ways already exists. He has often quoted the words of Pope John Paul II that 'effective communion requires affective communion'. In other words, friendship between the churches is the first small, but vital, step towards full communion.

Addressing the Anglican Synod at Chichester in 1978, Bishop Cormac stressed that the purpose of ecumenism 'is not just for the churches to come together, but rather that together they may give witness to Christ':

> How important it is to remember that, in the area of ecumenism, it is no longer the object to convert the other to one's own private view. The purpose of our meeting each other is not that the other turn from his wrong or wicked ways, but that each one of us should. The conversion we demand is our own, and that is painful.
>
> The scope of ecumenism is not like a merger of companies, with limits on how the merger will go. It is rather like a road which someone enters and from which he discovers there is no going back. It is a road we enter together and not one taken for our own sakes, but for the sake of all men. We enter it because we have experienced

a vision and a union with Christ. And [we have] a deep
belief that the Church exists to serve all people and not
just those who belong to it.

And speaking during his installation in Westminster Cathedral,
Archbishop Cormac recalled the scene in Canterbury Cathedral
in 1982 when Pope John Paul knelt in prayer with the Archbishop
of Canterbury:

> As I watched it, tears came to my eyes. I thought to
> myself, this is how it ought to be, this is how the enmi-
> ties, the misunderstandings, the hurt of the past must end
> – in common prayer, in a communion that is real, and in
> a common witness to the one Christ in whom we are
> already one.

In 1983 Bishop Cormac was appointed co-chairman of ARCIC II,
the second Anglican-Roman Catholic International Commission.
The first ARCIC had grown directly out of the historic meeting
between Archbishop Michael Ramsey and Pope Paul VI in 1966.
Encouraged by these men and their successors, over the next 30
years the commissions considered the doctrine of the Eucharist,
ministry and ordination, and authority in the Church.

Even here, Bishop Cormac was able to bring people together
as family. His co-chairman, Mark Santer, Anglican Bishop of
Birmingham, cites his 'ability to help people to feel comfortable
with each other and to trust one another'.

'Over those 16 years we became very close personal friends,'
says Bishop Santer. 'He's very good to work with. He has a gift
of getting the best out of people. He's a great encourager. One
of his greatest qualities is that, as well as being a priest, he's a
human being.

'The basis of our work in ARCIC was our common life as a
commission, eating together, our praying together, our enjoy-
ment in one another as human beings and our trust in one
another. He was a great one in facilitating that.'

One of the greatest stumbling blocks to the improving relationship between the churches came in 1992 when the Church of England Synod voted to allow women to be ordained priests, and the Catholic hierarchy of England & Wales expressed its 'profound regret' at the decision. But Bishop Cormac stressed that dialogue between the churches must continue: 'It cannot be denied that the question of women priests is a serious obstacle, but that doesn't mean, in the long term, that we are less committed. We can't expect instant solutions or instant overcoming of obstacles. But we can meet each other, work together and pray together.'

Many Anglican clergymen who didn't believe women *could* be ordained priests began converting to Catholicism, although their number was smaller than the mass exodus predicted by some newspapers. Many of those who converted asked about the possibility of becoming Catholic priests. Bishop Cormac was instrumental in the discussions with Rome that allowed these men, some of them married with children, to be ordained for Catholic ministry. It was expected that the Vatican would take up to a decade to produce a blueprint, but the decision was reached in just three years and Bishop Cormac, with his great understanding of the workings of both churches, is credited with having smoothed what could have been quite a stony path. As he said at the time:

> We are engaged in discerning God's will for each one of them. We are convinced that the ministry of these men, whether married or unmarried, will enrich the Church.
>
> The permission being given for the ordination of these married men is by way of exception and in recognition of the journey of faith which they have made. Such permission does not take away from the general norm of the Catholic Church which requires priests to live celibate lives.
>
> We have been asked by the Holy Father to be generous in our response to those of the Church of England who find themselves in difficulties of conscience. As bishops

we are confident that such generosity will be forthcoming and that we will be ready not only to welcome our new priests, and their wives and families, but also to be enriched by the experiences and insights which they will bring to us all.

Some of those men became priests of Arundel & Brighton Diocese and they, and their wives, all speak of the warm welcome they received from Bishop Cormac and from the whole diocesan family.

'The marvellous thing about Bishop Cormac is his wisdom,' said one man in his thirties who had been an Anglican priest for eight years before being received into the Catholic Church. 'All the way along the line everyone was treated as an individual. He's an incredibly sensitive and compassionate person. His wish for unity is as strong as anybody else's and that comes over. He sees that as absolutely essential to the Gospel.'

Father Brian Taylor, a married man with a long career in Anglican ministry, was ordained a priest for Arundel & Brighton Diocese in 1996, three years after he had been received into the Church. He said he immediately felt as though he belonged. 'We thought it would take about ten years to be settled in Rome but it all happened very quickly. There is a great feeling of belonging. I don't know how this compares with other Catholic dioceses because I've never belonged to one, but here there is a very great sense of belonging, something which I never experienced before in England. I had in Anglican ministry abroad, but not in England. Bishop Cormac is a team person. He's a rugger man – and you can't be a rugger man if you are not a team person.'

Despite the sensitive nature of these ordinations, Archbishop Cormac's involvement did nothing to diminish his good relationship with Church of England leaders. In 1999 the Archbishop of Canterbury, Dr George Carey, awarded him the Lambeth degree of Doctor of Divinity in recognition of his work for Christian unity in general and for Anglican-Roman Catholic relations in particular.

'Cormac's warmth, urbanity and generosity are almost a legend in ecumenical circles,' said Dr Carey. 'His hospitality at his gracious house in Storrington is also a legend. "A way of eating and drinking ourselves to visible unity", as Archbishop Habgood once put it.

'Cormac has worked tirelessly for many years for better ecumenical relations and I value and appreciate his stamina, his tenacity and his shrewd ability to find a constructive way forward. I greatly look forward to deepening our friendship and co-operation in future, on behalf of all those we seek to serve.'

Of course, even diocesan bishops need to relax and Archbishop Cormac's love of music, encouraged by Miss Hodges all those years ago, has always helped him to switch off from the pressures of diocesan life. He plays the piano at home and has even performed a piano concerto with full orchestra. Indeed, while his performance in the Clergy Revue in Brighton in June 1992 did much to help raise money for the Catholic aid agency, CAFOD, producers found it difficult to get him off stage once he had started. 'Archbishop Cormac has a real love of music,' says Clergy Revue co-ordinator Judith Rees. 'That really came over during the presentation that he did for us.' A polite way of saying that he would have played all night if they'd let him.

On those rare occasions when Archbishop Cormac can cast aside his skullcap and put his feet up in front of the telly, he enjoys watching sport, although he admits that his loyalties are split between three football clubs: Reading, Portsmouth and Brighton. 'Not that I am fickle, you understand,' he has explained. 'I was born in Reading, but I was a priest in Portsmouth, and now there is also a bit of my heart in Brighton.' All eyes will now be on the Archbishop to see if he chooses to offer his support to Arsenal or Spurs.

Having excelled at most sports in his youth, these days Archbishop Cormac mostly demonstrates his sporting prowess on the fairway. Many of his golfing partners are priests, although they deny the rumour that, in Arundel & Brighton diocese, promotion was based entirely on your handicap. Arundel Cathedral administrator Canon Anthony Whale describes

Archbishop Cormac as 'a good sportsman. I wouldn't say he plays enough to be good but it's just part of his relaxation.'

Canon Richard Incledon says that, for the Archbishop, playing golf is more than just a sporting or social occasion. 'Cormac enjoys his golf. But when he has a difficult proposal to put to a priest, if he wants him to go to some tricky job for example, he's quite likely to pop the question on the golf course.'

Not that he has had to persuade his priests very often. The late David Cashman – Arundel & Brighton's first bishop – once said that the one thing he wanted to see before his death, was his little diocese established as one where priest, people and bishop love and trust each other. According to many of the present priests in the diocese Bishop Cashman's wish was granted and Archbishop Cormac has built on those loving and trusting relationships.

Several of the Arundel & Brighton priests speak of Archbishop Cormac's impetuous nature and impulsive decisions and the fact that he doesn't always follow things through. Yet they have all tolerated these shortcomings. As one priest describes, 'we've all retained a great affection for him because his own goodness comes through'. For 22 years, Canon Incledon's old classmate was also his bishop and their friendship remains as firm now as it was in their student days.

'I'm not uncritical of him in things concerning administration of the diocese,' says Canon Incledon. 'But most of his faults he puts his finger on himself – impulsiveness, always new ideas. What he really needs is to clone himself and have the experience of being a parish priest under himself. There is an impulsiveness. He doesn't always remember what he's agreed, or even some particular appointment, but it didn't unduly matter. We have managed a happy relationship.

'We can be blunt about him and tell him home truths because we love him. Possibly because of my particular relationship I've been more conscious of the freedom. But I think any priest of the diocese would have had the same freedom and could have said what he liked to the bishop and know he would not get sent to a nasty parish the next day.'

Father Paul Jennings, a generation younger than Archbishop Cormac, agrees with Canon Incledon that his former boss is 'as much a friend as a bishop'.

'Archbishop Cormac is one who will always listen to advice,' he says. 'He may not always act upon it, but he is always open to thoughts and opinions, even if they do not correspond to his own. He is first and foremost a pastoral man, concerned very much for the well-being of his priests. He is someone in whom one can confide, someone ready to do whatever is in his power to help a priest in difficulties. He is clearly a man of deep personal faith, something he tries very hard to impart to others, particularly his priests.

'I don't recall him ever misusing his authority or being heavy-handed in his dealings with people. I've never known him stand on ceremony and I think he would probably be quite embarrassed if anyone did. But he knows exactly what the role of the Church is in society today. He knows exactly where he wants to go and where he thinks the Church should go.'

Father Tony Churchill recalls having to miss an important meeting with the Bishop as his mother was dying. Bishop Cormac simply delayed the meeting and went straight to Mrs Churchill's bedside. 'He had met her before but he didn't really know her. And he had gone out of his way to come to us. He said some prayers and gave her a blessing. It was a lovely thing to do and it was above and beyond the call of duty.'

Similarly, when Father Peter Edwards's father was terminally ill, Bishop Cormac sought out the dying man's address and sent him a personal letter thanking Mr Edwards, whom he had never met, for his son's ministry. 'It strikes me that Bishop Cormac took time out to trace my parents' address and to write a personal letter,' says Father Edwards. And when Father Edwards's mother, who was then living with her son and working as his housekeeper, contracted Alzheimer's, Bishop Cormac insisted that Mrs Edwards remain in the presbytery where she was cared for by volunteers in the parish. Following Mrs Edwards's death, the Bishop personally thanked the parishioners for the help and support they had given their priest during this difficult time.

'As a priest I have always felt that if I had any crisis or difficulty, I could talk to Bishop Cormac,' says Father Edwards. 'Whenever you went to see him at his home in Storrington it was always very informal. He's very clever too. He has the charm. If you were seeing him for an appointment or something like that, he would say things like "You know you're going to the best parish in the diocese, Father."'

Father Churchill says Archbishop Cormac has always encouraged his priests in their studies, publishing a varied list of suggested reading material in his *Ad Clerums*, the regular letter sent out by a bishop to the clergy of his diocese. 'He has made it possible for all sorts of men to go and do further studies,' he says. 'The result is that he leaves a diocese with a lot of men well qualified.'

Of course, the overall feeling of the people of Arundel & Brighton diocese is that they would prefer it if their bishop wasn't leaving at all. 'Since his appointment to Westminster, I have not heard anyone say other than that he will be missed in the diocese and that their gain is our loss,' says Father Paul Jennings.

Canon Incledon believes that change will be good for Archbishop Cormac and that, despite taking on a demanding new appointment at an age when most lay people have retired, 'He will respond naturally to the occasion that calls forth his energies.'

'There have been moments when he has said he was feeling his age,' says Canon Incledon. 'But I suspect that a complete change will revive his energies. Maybe, had he stayed with us, he would have gone on in the countdown to retirement. He is basically very healthy – I don't think he's had a day in hospital since he had his appendix out in his teens. There are times when he looks awfully tired. Sometimes his colour is too high, sometimes he just looks exhausted – and then he bobs up again. You can see him almost straighten up and regain energy.'

As far back as 1986 Lord Longford, in his book *The Bishops*, had described the then Bishop of Arundel & Brighton as 'often tipped as the natural successor to Cardinal Hume as Archbishop of Westminster'. Bishop Cormac was as surprised as everyone else when, on 13 February 2000, the *Sunday Times* announced that

Pope John Paul had appointed him to the post. Several London churches, believing the report to be true, began praying for their new archbishop, and one even held a champagne breakfast. But Archbishop Cormac quickly issued a statement stressing that he knew nothing about the appointment.

It might have been worth placing a bet with Ladbrokes, who had been offering odds of 25 to 1, for two days later the formal announcement was made that Cardinal Hume's successor would indeed be Cormac Murphy-O'Connor. The Archbishop-elect reiterated the fact that he had been the last to know but said that 'although I am not as young as I was when I first became a bishop, I now undertake this new task with equal willingness'.

Father Brian is 'impressed' by the way his younger brother has taken on the burdens of a new appointment. 'Cormac is at peace with himself,' he says, 'and that is going to be very helpful for him in the months and the years to come. He has had 22 years as a bishop, so he is not without experience. I'm fairly certain he'll be able to cope.'

On taking up office, Archbishop Cormac stressed that there would be no great changes in Westminster archdiocese but immediately added that 'there is much to be done and I accept very willingly the challenges that lie ahead because I know that with the help of God and the active co-operation of priests and people, we can fulfil what Christ, the Son of God, wants us to do and to be'.

This impulsive man, who is constantly thinking up new ways of spreading the Gospel, has left his old diocese with one such initiative unfinished. Preparations had been well under way for Arundel & Brighton's first diocesan synod in 2002. The parishes were already looking at the problems of how best to employ human and financial resources, future mission, social justice and the challenges of a secular society. It was, said Bishop Cormac, 'a pilgrimage reaching into the third millennium' and an opportunity 'to reform and reshape the diocese'.

At the moment, Arundel & Brighton is waiting to hear who will be Bishop Cormac's successor. Perhaps the new man will take the idea down from the shelf, dust it off and set it back in motion.

He might have other ideas of his own. Perhaps Archbishop Cormac will consider a similar scheme in his new diocese. But contrary to reports in certain newspapers, the people of Westminster Archdiocese can be sure of one thing: Archbishop Cormac is not a mere caretaker, he is not there just to keep an eye on things until he retires and a younger man takes over.

Canon Peter Humfrey laughs at the suggestion. 'I don't think he'll lie down and do nothing,' says Canon Humfrey, who has worked with Archbishop Cormac for many years. 'He has an enormously strong constitution, he lives a regular life and he's done that for years. He has a tremendous workload and has the stamina.

'And there is one thing Cormac was particularly good at: where there were controversial issues, or issues which were difficult to resolve pastorally, he seemed by some genius to be able to find a pastoral solution which went beyond just dealing with the problem. He was very good at dealing with things like ecumenical matters and marriage cases, areas which have a legal side but a bigger pastoral aspect.

'I would like to think that his genius in having a very forward-looking pastoral solution to problems would affect what he does at Westminster and perhaps have a national effect as well.'

Or, as another Arundel & Brighton priest puts it, 'Cormac isn't a man to sit and watch the grass grow – and we sometimes wish he would.'

Archbishop Bowen's presidency of the Bishops' Conference comes to an end in November 2000 and, according to precedent, it's likely, although not inevitable, that Archbishop Cormac will be elected in his place. And with several dioceses looking for new leaders over the next year or so, the face of the Bishops' Conference is likely to change substantially. If Archbishop Cormac's thirst for new ways of doing things shakes up the way the Conference works, he is sure to take his brother bishops with him for, as one of them has already pointed out, 'Cormac is more of a team player than Cardinal Hume.'

In other words, Archbishop Cormac is a man of energy and enthusiasm who is constantly thinking of ways to improve the Church's mission in the world and, sometimes annoyingly, constantly challenging people to join him in that work. Perhaps one day the Archdiocese of Westminster really will need a new broom, for it seems their recently installed archbishop is likely to kick up quite a bit of dust. As he said the day his appointment was announced, 'there is much to be done and I accept very willingly the challenges that lie ahead. I know that with the help of God and the active co-operation of priests and people, we can fulfil what Christ the Son of God wants us to do and to be. Collaboration has always been foremost in my ministry so far and it will continue to be so in the years ahead.'

There's no doubt that Archbishop Cormac will be greatly missed by his old diocesan family of Arundel & Brighton. But there's one person in particular who will miss him, and that's Max, the elderly golden retriever, who knows and loves the new Archbishop of Westminster better than anyone else. For years they have walked together on the South Downs above St Joseph's Hall at Storrington and all the recent fuss has left Max, who is not by nature a media hound, feeling rather confused.

Max lives in a basket near the kitchen and there's a whole team of nuns who prepare his favourite tidbits. (The sisters make a mean shepherd's pie and Max looks forward to any episcopal leftovers.) After weighing up the options, Max felt he just wouldn't be as happy on the mean streets of London. So before he left Arundel & Brighton diocese, Archbishop Cormac made one last, and most important, episcopal appointment and entrusted Father Tony Barry, his secretary for many years, with the job of looking after his old canine pal.

✠

2. The Way We Were

Archbishop Cormac has left a diocese where the average weekly Mass attendance is three or four per cent above the national average. Even so, he has not been complacent and, in launching the Arundel & Brighton Diocesan Synod originally scheduled for 2002, he stressed that 'with fewer clergy we will need to reflect on our current structures'. He asked his people to consider how limited finances and resources could best be used 'in supporting parishes and in providing for the real needs of people'.

He has already been charged with the job of 'stemming the exodus' from the pews both by the national press and by groups within the Church. It hardly seems fair to lay this task on the shoulders of one man when evangelization is the duty of all Christians, lay and ordained. But there's no doubt that the pews are emptying at an alarming rate and, although there are plenty of people willing to complain about the fact and lay blame at other people's feet, nobody has yet come up with a practical solution to reverse the trend.

There was a time when Catholics crowded into their churches. Whole families, from toddlers to truculent 18-year-olds, went to Sunday Mass together fearing eternal damnation – or the more immediate wrath of their parents – if they did not. Deliberately missing Mass was a mortal sin and if you died in a state of mortal sin you were no longer guaranteed a place among the elect. White nighties, halos and harps were not for those who couldn't be bothered getting out of bed on a Sunday morning. And you had to fast from midnight in order to receive Communion, so all those who had snatched a piece of breakfastorial toast would remain in their pews during the procession to the altar rail.

At High Mass only the most devout, those who had managed without food for up to 12 hours, would receive Communion. At the back of the church, teenage lads ejected from their beds with the threat that 'you'll go as long as you live in this house …' would stay in church for the minimum time before diving out to the parish club for a pint or two. These were the days when Catholics only had to stay at Mass from the Gospel until the priest's Communion in order to fulfil their 'obligation' to 'hear' Sunday Mass.

When the elderly parish priest eventually joined them at the bar he would be treated with the utmost reverence – and quite a few drams – by those who had slept through his sermon. If he was encountered in the street, caps would be touched and fore-locks tugged.

These were the days when even the least devout treated the accoutrements of their religion with a certain amount of respect. It was a great time for statistics – the pews were full and the collection plate contained enough pennies for massive school and church building programmes. It was a golden age that lasted a little over a century, from the restoration of the hierarchy in 1850 to the great exodus from the pews that began in the late 1960s.

There are those who believe that Catholic churches emptied as a direct result of the Second Vatican Council in general, and the coming of the English Mass in particular. The only way to test the idea is to rerun ecclesiastical history while maintaining the Latin Tridentine rite – and watch the churches empty even faster. For it seems unlikely that the psychedelic generation would have stayed any longer because of the ancient liturgy, unless someone was burning pot in the thurible.

Theologian and *Catholic Times* columnist Father Francis Marsden believes the truth lies in the fact that the Church was having to cope with many outside influences at the time. 'Society was secularizing, paganizing really, at the very time Catholicism was opening the window to the world,' he says. 'Having grown up in the ghetto, with a lot of "Thou Shalt Nots", and because the older priests had been in such a closed world, when the windows were thrown open some of them kicked over the traces. A lot of things came into the Church and there wasn't the experience or the discernment to sort out what was consonant with the Gospel and what was anti the Gospel. So people went haywire at times.'

Father Marsden describes himself as a traditionalist, but he has little sympathy with the reactionary wing of the Church that blames today's problems entirely on the workings of Vatican II. His complaint is simply that the baby was thrown out with the bath water, that the Church 'dumbed down' in the years following the Council and no longer presented its people with challenges. Unlike Jews and Muslims, Catholics no longer appeared to hold different values from the rest of society.

'We live in a culture of convenience and luxury,' says Father Marsden, 'and the Church should have been standing out against that and saying, for example, "keep to the laws of fasting". It just seemed to endorse the trend of society, saying we no longer needed to fast on a Friday. Everything that seems to have been done, seems to have been to make life easy, to have gone along with society. And, in fact, if you go too far down that road then people say, "Oh, we can do what we like, can't we." We were taught in the past that sex before marriage was out but it seems we can change anything now. That was a failure to distinguish between Church discipline and eternal moral law.'

It was certainly confusing for people who'd been brought up to believe that the old Tridentine Mass would never change and that eating meat on a Friday was tantamount to a mortal sin. As Michael Carson's anti-hero Martin Benson declares in *Yanking Up the Yo-Yo*:

> The goal posts are being shifted. When I was growing up everything seemed so hard and so fast. I took everything I was told literally because that's how I was told to take it. My indoctrination won't allow me to pick and choose. I have to take all or nothing. And I can't take it all.

Despite all the upheaval of Vatican II – everything from the new liturgy to nuns showing their ankles and enjoying their first perms – it was the document *Humanae Vitae* that caused many Catholics to rethink their position. It had been expected that the Pontifical Commission investigating contraception would recommend some forms of artificial family planning as acceptable. But when Pope Paul VI's most famous – or infamous – document was eventually published it was a definite NO. For the first time ordinary Catholics either ignored the teaching of *Humanae Vitae* and carried on practising their faith – and contraception – or left the Church altogether without fear of divine reprisal. As David Lodge notes in *How Far Can You Go?*:

> At some point in the nineteen-sixties, Hell disappeared. No one could say for certain when this happened. First it was there, then it wasn't. On the whole, the disappearance of Hell was a great relief, though it brought new problems.

Michael Carson and David Lodge are, of course, writing novels. But both men were growing through the changes in the Church and their fictional characters summarize the feelings of many Catholics of the time.

The world was changing and many people, young people in particular, were looking for new experiences. A Church that appeared to be authoritarian – and that had taught many of the flower people with straps, canes and slippers – was unlikely to appeal to a generation seeking free love and free expression. Statistics show that it was the teenagers of the sixties who disappeared from the Catholic Church but what effect the Second Vatican Council, and Pope John XXIII's attempts to let a little fresh air into the Church had, we will never really know.

It's not just the Church that's suffered over the last 30 years. The monarchy, Parliament and the police have all become targets of scepticism. Institutions that were once considered beyond criticism have become Aunt Sallies in the national coconut shy. The days when you doffed your cap to the parish priest were also the days when you didn't dare look sideways at the village bobby. The days when you kneeled in awe before the tabernacle or bowed your head at the mention of the name Jesus, were the days when everybody stood for the national anthem in cinemas and theatres. The days when all Catholic children attended Catholic schools were the days when most people who were eligible to vote at the general election exercised their right to do so – although they might have heeded Father's warnings about the dangers of socialism.

'Institutions and their representatives now find themselves living in the X-ray environment created by the modern news media,' explains Dr Jim McDonnell, director of the Catholic Communications Centre. 'Under such persistent media gaze, institutions have had to face up to the fact that they can no longer take their authority or credibility for granted. For an institution like the Catholic Church this realization has come slowly and been particularly hard to bear.

'Institutions that claim moral and spiritual authority and the right to offer guidance not only to individuals but to society generally are particularly vulnerable in such an environment. For the Church it is crucially important that the gap between the ideal and the actual, the appearance and reality, should be as narrow as possible. Credibility is easily lost and hardly won.'

It's certainly true that the Church is no longer just the target of gentle joshing, as in the days of TV series like *Oh Brother* and *Bless Me, Father*, but is now open to hostile criticism from the tabloids. How many people have not bought a copy of the *News of the World* because yet another clergyman has run away with his housekeeper or fled to the United States following accusations of sex with altar boys?

It's not that society no longer has sacred cows. Try attending a dinner party in the smarter suburbs and admitting you still like eating dead animals and you'll be shot down by a volley of abuse. Suggest that Tony Blair isn't God and you risk a good splattering with the nut meringue gateau. And it's a brave man indeed who would suggest, in mixed company, that Punch & Judy is just harmless fun or that women can't be priests.

Atheists and sitcom writers aside, those who are quick to criticize the Christian churches in general and the Catholic Church in particular – tales of convent school repression are always good for a laugh – appear to be searching for something. Transubstantiation, celibacy and statues might be considered signs of a patriarchal, authoritarian Church, but there's a noticeable growth in the number of meditation tapes for sale, the number of healers setting up business and the number of 'alternative' therapies of every description. A generation that has never heard plainsong or smelled incense in church is sending CDs of medieval music frisbeeing high up in the crossover charts and filling its homes with candles and sweet-smelling aromas.

'It's what they used to get from the Church,' says the writer Alice Thomas Ellis. 'It's what they used to get from the Mass and from Benediction. It was nourishing and it was all taken away from them. What we had was nourishment for the soul and then some weird puritanism came along – and it's all to do with ecumenism and being more protestant than the Protestants, who never made the remotest move in our direction.

'The whole heart and soul of the Church is the Eucharist and when they started messing about with that, sidelining it and pretending it was really of no importance, a lot of people failed to see the light any more. They thought "Well, stuff this" and they went somewhere else.

'The words have been altered so radically in some cases that it doesn't have anything like the same meaning or sense. "Say but the word and my soul shall be healed" is now "Say but the word and I shall be healed", which is totally different. All sorts of things like that have happened, and now they're surprised that they can't get bums on seats.'

Sister Margaret O'Ryan, a 70-year-old nun living in a tower block on the outskirts of Liverpool, believes people are searching to fill a void in their lives. 'There's a space for God in each one of us. If you don't fill it with God then you're going to fill it with something else because you've got to. You can't leave that vacuum. That's why people are after drugs, that's why they're after sex. They are finding one thing after another doesn't satisfy them because they're not rooted in something. You need roots, you need something to go back to.'

Addressing the opening session of the University of Sussex in October 1980, Archbishop Cormac said that 'everyone has a religious instinct and it's not always easy to describe it':

> It comes to one at different times in one's life: a kind of sense of bafflement in face of the unknown; a kind of seeking after the beyond. It may come to us as a sense of wonder and a capacity to appreciate and respond to the beautiful.
>
> If we are talking about the real things of life we should not forget that the instinct for God, the quest for God, is in each one of us. There are people who will say that this primeval instinct for the beyond is bound up with fear, with the need for security, or a search for a fatherlike figure. There are all these things, but my belief, like that of countless millions of others throughout the ages, is that there is a purpose, a meaning and a destiny for man and the world, and that purpose is bound up with the existence of a personal God, whom, in however small a measure, we can know and adore and have contact with.

A survey published in October 1999 claimed that a growing number of Britons were searching for a spiritual life but were turning to alternative medicine and alternative religion rather than to the mainstream churches.

Of course you can do anything with statistics – but some of the figures published towards the end of the last millennium (or century, or year – take your pick) were, to say the least, alarming. Inspired perhaps by the 'fin de siècle' feeling, statistics poured out of every publication from September to New Year, detailing everything from the top 100 songs of the century to the exodus from the pews of all denominations.

A *Sunday Times* survey showed it was businessmen and financiers who wielded the most influence among the British, with Church leaders coming so far down the list that they hardly registered. A November Gallup poll showed the British to be the least religious people in the world. In December the English Church Survey had shown that British Christianity was 'in crisis' and that churches might be empty by 2020 unless something was done to stem the tide. According to the survey, Sunday attendance across all Christian denominations fell from 4.7 million in 1989 to 3.7 million in 1998, a drop of 22 per cent, while the number of older worshippers increased from 900,000 to 950,000 during the same period.

By the time the century came to its spectacular firework finale, yet another survey, this time commissioned by the *Daily Telegraph*, showed that few people had any idea what the millennium festivities were actually celebrating. And it wasn't just the heathens. A third of the so-called Christians questioned could not name a single one of the Gospels and more than half said they only went to church for 'christenings, weddings and funerals'. No wonder that the Archbishop of Canterbury described Britain as having 'an allergy' to religion.

So much for religion in general, but what about Catholicism in particular? It seems that the barque of St Peter – and England, the Dowry of Mary, in particular – had also finally hit a rock or two by the end of the second millennium. Specifically Catholic surveys showed similar results to those of what Catholics used to call 'our separated brethren'. There had been encouraging signs, with growing numbers of people being received into the Church at Easter throughout the 1990s – but this in no way compensated for the numbers who were 'lapsing' from practice of their faith. It was, according to the *Catholic Times*, 'the worst crisis since the Reformation'.

While Mass attendance figures were dropping, the numbers of those attending Confession were plummeting. In November 1999 Archbishop Julian Herranz, the Vatican's top legal expert, reminded Catholics worldwide that the Church expects those 'who have violated any of God's commandments' to 'purify themselves of the sin through the sacrament of penance before approaching eucharistic Communion'. The following month the bishops of England & Wales announced they were preparing a 'penance pack' to help people celebrate the Jubilee Year – in other words, they were hoping to encourage return to Confession.

Back in 1982 Archbishop Cormac had commented on the decline of Confession, and, in a Lenten pastoral letter, had appealed to his people to make more use of the sacrament:

> Many Catholics do not use the sacrament of penance as they once did. Indeed for many people it is a long, long time since they frequented the sacrament. When we go to Confession we admit that we have sinned before God and our neighbour. We admit that we do not, as a Church, as witnesses to Christ, live up to his gospel and his teaching. In this sense my sins not only offend God and my neighbour, but the Church itself. They not only affect my relationships with God and with my neighbour, but also affect the Church, and the more we love the Church, the more we see the damage done to her by sin.

The turn-of-the-century Counting of Catholics began in earnest in 1999 with a survey in the *Westminster Record* – later published in *The Tablet* – that showed a drop in Mass attendance from 2.1 million in 1964 to less than 1.1 million in 1998. The most interesting statistic in the piece showed the widening gulf between the estimated number of Catholics and the number who actually attended Mass.

The late Archbishop Derek Worlock used to argue the benefits of quality over quantity – in other words it's better to have a church half full of people who have made a positive decision to practise their faith than a church full of people attending through fear of eternal damnation.

Alice Thomas Ellis disagrees. 'I don't think they were there out of fear. This is the spin they all put on it and it's a load of old garbage. They completely misrepresent the way the Church used to be. There used to be great devotion. The churches were very pleasant places to go because they hadn't all been stripped and reordered. There was colour, there was warmth, there was a feeling of reverence and sanctity – there was the sanctuary light gleaming, there were candles, flowers and incense.

'Whenever people change things they have to represent the past as dreadful and it's total misrepresentation, a complete distortion of the way things were. The town planners ripped the heart out of cities like Liverpool and then, as far as I'm concerned, the Church ripped the heart out of Catholicism.'

Daphne McLeod, chairman of traditionalist group Pro Ecclesia et Pontifice, agrees that 'the supernatural and the spiritual are being played down too much'.

'We have human needs. The church used to supply them and, now it's not, people look somewhere else because they need it,' she says. 'If you go to a Latin Mass now you'll find it packed. It's the spirituality that draws the young people – it's certainly not nostalgia because they don't remember it. But they come in crowds and they bring their young families. And the children behave a lot better. Because there's such an atmosphere it gets through even to little children and they are quiet and still, whereas if you go to a *Novus Ordo* [the modern Mass] children can be fidgety and quite difficult. When we were children we didn't fidget because we had the Tridentine Mass.'

Like Alice Thomas Ellis, Daphne McLeod is saddened by the argument of 'quality over quantity'. 'It upsets me, because every human soul is of immense importance – we are all quality. The Lord died for each one of us. You can't dismiss people and say they don't matter. Everyone matters. If the people are there they show they love our Lord. If the people are not there they are making a statement that they don't want to be there.'

The National Catholic Directory 2000, published days before the turn of the century, confirmed that just over 25 per cent of the Catholics in England & Wales were churchgoers, or at least had gone to church on the day the census was taken. This percentage was roughly the same as the previous year's but the estimated number of Catholics had dropped – so there were now approximately 30,000 fewer people attending Catholic churches than there had been. That might only be an average of 12 people per parish but translate it into the amount of money churchgoers put on the collection plate and the crisis deepens. If that dozen people each give £5 every week they're donating more than £3,000 a year – enough to feed a priest, or fix the leaking roof, or repair the school hall. In financial terms, Catholic parishes have lost enough people over the last few years to have to reconsider where their now limited resources are best spent.

At the beginning of Advent 1999, the Archdiocese of Westminster announced a Jehovah's Witness-style recruitment campaign. Bishop Vincent Nichols, diocesan administrator since Cardinal Hume's death, invited his people to renew contact with the thousands of Catholics who had drifted away from the Church by travelling around in pairs and literally knocking on doors.

In Lancaster diocese, Bishop John Brewer issued a pastoral letter urging his flock to 'take stock' of the situation and consider 'how well or how poorly we live our faith'. He announced that the number of Mass-goers had halved in just 15 years and spoke of the falling numbers of children who would continue to practise their faith after primary school: 'We all have our own explanations for why this is happening. It is easy to blame others for what they may or may not be doing. A much more Christian response is to ask myself what can I do to strengthen and renew the faith I love.'

Whenever bishops issue a rallying call they are – we hope – thinking pastorally rather than fiscally. But in the Catholic Church the two are, to a significant extent, inseparable and 'bums on seats' (to quote Alice Thomas Ellis) really do count – you can't feed your priest or heat your church without money in the bank. In Germany people who claim to belong to a religious denomination pay church tax direct from their salary. Whether or not they attend their chosen church, they still provide the cash for its upkeep and for many of the social services run by the churches. In Britain Catholicism must survive solely on voluntary donations from those who attend their local church. And diocesan bishops are responsible for making sure that money is spent wisely. It's all very well funding a building that has 'always been there' but any bishop who pours pennies into an empty building is not exactly practising prudent stewardship.

It was for this reason that Archbishop Patrick Kelly decided to close St Joseph's College, Upholland, in response to the 'signs of the times'. Liverpool's former seminary had been used for all sorts of diocesan activities, but was becoming far too expensive to maintain in a diocese which once had the biggest Mass attendance figures in the country but which was now considering the closure of formerly packed churches.

'I have decided that we should no longer use the buildings at Upholland,' Archbishop Kelly announced on Home Mission Sunday, 1999:

> It would not be impossible to finance their continued use. If we were prepared to set aside many other diocesan developments and activities, the money could certainly be found. Careful note has been taken of the actual use made of the buildings, and we have found that, given their size and the amount of work and money expended on them, the usage has been very small. I am not free to use the Archdiocese's resources in any way I please. I may use them only in the way that will most effectively initiate and develop enterprises which strengthen us all as disciples and heralds of the Lord.

In other words Liverpool's Catholics could no longer afford to maintain what had become a white elephant. As recently as 1967 new classrooms were built at Upholland to house the growing number of student priests and junior seminarians. But those were the days when the churches were bursting at the seams and there were plenty of donations to pay for the training of the many young men coming forward to serve the archdiocese. By 1999 the building was no longer used as a seminary and had proved too large for other attempted uses.

Across the river from Liverpool, neighbouring Shrewsbury diocese had announced similar financial problems. There were explanations that the diocese had more churches than were strictly necessary and that there weren't enough priests to staff them. In truth, there are easily enough priests for Mass to be celebrated regularly in all the churches – in England & Wales there are currently just under 5,600 secular priests and just over 3,600 parish churches. The reality is that the smaller numbers attending mean there isn't enough cash to maintain large barn-like buildings constructed in an earlier era, when each parish had four or five large congregations every Sunday and when even the pennies of the poor added up to sufficient income for the maintenance of church, schools and three or four priests.

Shrewsbury published a 'green paper' suggesting that a number of churches would close and some parishes would be amalgamated. Some churches would become Mass centres while others would be demolished or sold off. Bishop Brian Noble said the plan was to ensure that 'the life and mission of the Church in our diocese will continue and develop' but added that 'if this is to happen significant changes will have to be made'.

'Careful deployment of our clergy will be necessary,' he said. 'Nor can we afford to be spending all our declining resources on property. We are one family and our resources must be available for the benefit of all. Change is never easy but the option of remaining as we are is simply not open to us.'

A similar consultation process was launched in Hexham & Newcastle diocese while, at the same time, it was revealed that Catholics in Nottingham diocese's Peak District were already being served by peripatetic priests.

Monsignor Kieran Conry, head of the Catholic Media Office, points out that it is population shift, not just the fall in numbers, which is the problem. As city centres have emptied and new towns have been built, parish boundaries have remained roughly the same and too many of our churches are now in the wrong place.

'In the early seventies the number of priests in England and Wales peaked at 7,600,' he says. 'We're now down to 5,600. In that time the number of parishes has remained the same. So we have 2,000 fewer priests and we're still having to run the same number of parishes.'

Again, as Monsignor Conry says, you can do almost anything with statistics and counting the Mass-going population one Sunday per year doesn't provide a full picture. 'You're assuming that everybody there that day goes to Mass every Sunday but that's not clear at all. Research done in a parish in Norwood, in south London, showed that from a weekly Mass attendance of 600 there were in reality about 1,000 people going to Mass, but it meant that these 1,000 people were not going every week. And that's clear from independent research too.

'People have a different regard to rules and authority today so they make their own decision about whether they want to go to Mass or not. They are still being told to go to Mass on Sunday but they are not listening.'

Monsignor Conry is keen to stress that, compared to many other nations, the British still don't have too many problems finding a priest to celebrate Mass for them. 'The ratio of priests to population per capita is one of the highest in the world. There's a billion Catholics worldwide and most of those do not go to Mass on Sunday – Mass is not available because there is no priest for them. And here we talk about being inconvenienced because we only have three Masses to choose from. We've got to use manpower – and it is all right to use "*man*power" in this sense – more effectively, more economically.'

The third millennium of Christianity began with the announcement by the Bishops' Conference of England & Wales that a working party would be set up to look at the problem of church resources nationwide and that Shrewsbury's 'green paper' would be used as a model for other dioceses to consider.

If we are to believe all those dreaded statistics, the golden age of British Catholicism is, if not dead, then at least lying dormant. We can no longer presume that people will pour into our churches and pile enough money into the collection plate to build schools and maintain churches. The dioceses that are re-evaluating their fiscal policies are doing so because they have no choice. Even though many Catholics grow particularly fond of their churches, it is people, not buildings that matter. However painful, the 'crisis' must be sorted and sorted soon or, instead of inheriting a well-ordered Church, our children will receive nothing more than dozens of crumbling buildings.

Speaking on Radio 2's *Good Morning Sunday* the week his election was announced, Archbishop Cormac stressed that the 'quality of Christian life' was vital in attracting people to the Church.

> The way in which people actually live out their Christian life and witness to it is the most important thing. The question of 'getting people back to Church' has something to do with the way believers live out their faith and, at a certain point, you've got to leave it to God. Those who believe in Jesus Christ and follow him, and give a real witness in our society, will in fact make new converts to the faith in Jesus Christ.

✠

3. The Hope of Tomorrow?

At his installation Mass, Archbishop Cormac asked the congregation to consider 'What kind of vision are we giving the young
people in our society today?' In other words, instead of spending
time and energy criticizing the younger generation, we should be
asking ourselves what example we are setting, what sort of hopes
and aspirations we have for them:

> I believe that there are values which the vast majority
> of people in our countries in their heart of heart share.
> And these values and truths need to be heard with ever-
> increasing strength. As I look out at our society I see
> many things that give me joy. I see young people with
> great ideals for building a better world, who try to live
> many of the ideals of the Kingdom of God.
>
> Every summer for the last 22 years I have taken a
> large group of people to Lourdes, including many young
> people. There I see them engaged in prayer, in caring for
> the sick, enjoying each other's company as a community
> of faith. And it is as if they have a new lung with which to
> breathe and new eyes with which to see.

While Archbishop Cormac is encouraged by this sight, you only
have to turn back to the statisticians to find a rather more gloomy
picture. It is estimated that up to 92 per cent of young people

leaving Catholic schools also abandon the practice of their religion. Considering there are more than 750,000 youngsters currently being educated in Catholic schools in England & Wales, it would appear that few of them practise their religion during their schooldays either. This can present a challenge for parish priests preparing young children for the sacraments of Communion and Reconciliation and can also be a headache for religious education teachers who discover that, unlike in days gone by, they cannot presume any sort of Catholic basis on which to build.

In October 1999 Father Richard Moroney, parish priest of St Anthony's, Slough, announced that children who did not come to Mass were not eligible to prepare for their first Communion. His argument was simple: first Communion is centred around the Mass and if children and their parents had no real experience of Mass-going then there was little chance he would be able to teach them what first Communion was all about. This was not, he insists, an attempt to bribe lapsed parents back into the Church. He simply wanted them to be honest.

'I said that in order for the children to get on to the next stage of initiation in the Church, to receive the sacraments of Reconciliation and Communion, they already needed to have been taught to pray by their parents, to have some knowledge of Jesus from their parents and to be introduced to the liturgical life of the Church by their parents,' Father Moroney explains. 'That's all. I said "If this hasn't been done, do not put your children forward for enrolment in the sacrament of Reconciliation or first Communion."'

Some parents ran to the press, claiming that the sins of the fathers were being visited upon the next generation, but Father Moroney denies that children were being blamed for their parents' lack of practice. He stresses that parents are free to bring up their children as they want, but if they want to bring them up as Catholics there are certain requirements.

'I'm not saying that if parents start coming to Mass their children can receive the sacraments,' he says. 'I'm saying they already need to have been doing this. This is the prerequisite. I want the word to get around right from baptism onwards that they have a duty. They may get into a Catholic school because their children have been baptized, but that doesn't give them a right to any other sacrament of initiation unless they've done their work with the child.'

Father Moroney is offering neither a threat nor a promise. He insists that his actions are not intended to bring lapsed parents back to the pews for the sake of their children. He simply wants parents to be honest about their own beliefs and intentions. 'I was asking them not to confuse their children by having a split between practice and reality. I didn't want the abuse that was going on to continue without me saying something about it and laying down what the Church teaches. My business is to preach the Gospel and to say how the Church views things. But the Church does not enter into any condemnation – if you honestly don't believe, you don't have to believe.'

Daphne McLeod, a retired primary school headteacher as well as chairman of Pro Ecclesia et Pontifice, believes the problem of lapsed parents and ignorant children is a direct result of three generations of children being taught badly in Catholic schools. She is convinced that by basing all primary school religious education (RE) on the *Catechism of the Catholic Church*, the pews will be full in no time at all.

'Children will respond to the Truth,' she says. 'We've always had some children from homes that didn't practise, even right back in the forties when I started teaching, but they were still won over by the Truth. I remember little children who would take themselves to Mass because they had been taught the faith in school.

'You don't write them off because the parents don't go to Mass, you teach them the faith, properly and effectively, you wait to see what happens and, with God's grace, a lot of good will happen.

'The schools can't make them into good Catholics – that needs practice at home – but the school can teach them just as it teaches them chemistry or history. Our children are not only not practising, they are ignorant. They don't know the first thing about the Catholic faith. I shall die before anyone teaches the Truth in this country but I do hope it will happen one day.'

These are strong words but they are just the tip of the iceberg. The row over what should and shouldn't be taught in Catholic RE lessons has raged for years and has come to a head in the last decade.

Bishop Vincent Nichols went some way towards lancing this festering boil when, at the end of 1999, he invited comments from priests, teachers, parents and pupils on the general state of religious education in the Catholic classrooms of England & Wales. Following the introduction of the textbooks *Here I Am* for primary schools and *Weaving the Web* for secondaries, there had been several years of unrest about Catholic RE. These two schemes, claimed their opponents, were far from Catholic. They didn't include the basic Catholic beliefs and treated other faiths as being of equal importance. Their defenders responded that they were only intended as source material that an experienced Catholic teacher could draw upon. But the fact that many dioceses had recommended these books as the official text for their schools left many people wondering what was going on. So both the exponents of modern catechetics and the more traditionalist opposition welcomed the fact that RE was at last being widely discussed.

According to the results of this survey, published in January 2000, RE should 'nurture and deepen the Christian life given in baptism and support parents in their role as the primary teachers of the faith'. The provision of good syllabuses and 'quality RE programmes' was seen as vital, as was the need for teachers to be professionally trained for their work and to live 'their own life of faith, hope and love'. A working knowledge of the Catholic faith based on scripture and theology was important but there was also the recognition that any scheme should involve home, school and parish working together.

Daphne McLeod is the first to admit that she has been a thorn in the sides of bishops and catechists alike. A softly spoken woman, she is not afraid to tell the bishops exactly what she thinks of RE schemes like *Here I Am* and *Weaving the Web*.

There have been attempts to silence her – even a threat of legal action – but Mrs McLeod remains undaunted, believing it is her duty to expose error. 'I don't want to be nasty but you have to expose what's happening,' she says. 'They don't like their short-comings being exposed but you can't let the children suffer like this without saying anything.'

Her belief that Catholic schools should base all their curriculums directly on the Catechism leads her to insist that all modern Catholic RE schemes should be scrapped. 'It is the Divine Truth revealed by our Lord which is exactly what is not being taught, the Truth the Church has preserved for us ever since and which, until now, has been passed on from one generation to the next. Now in this country we've stopped doing it and that means the Church will end in this country unless it's put right.'

In fact, she is willing to go further and claims that there is a deliberate policy 'in every diocese in this country not to teach the Faith in either secondary or primary schools. If you look at the textbooks the bishops are giving them you'll see they are teaching error – they won't teach original sin, the fall, the need for redemption, grace, all the basic things that are part of our faith.

'We are cheating our children. We are letting them down right, left and centre and the only way to get it right is to expose it. So I spend my time trying to expose it and make myself very unpopular, but you can't just do nothing when this is happening.'

Canon Peter Humfrey is the National Advisor for Religious Education and Catechesis. A priest in Archbishop Cormac's old diocese of Arundel & Brighton, he advises the Bishops' Conference on religious education in schools and has, therefore, been involved in revisions to both the primary and secondary school syllabuses. He is keen to refute accusations that the bishops are going out of the way to teach what Mrs McLeod describes as 'error'.

'The bishops are teaching the Catholic faith and they are teaching the Catholic faith which is handed to us through the Catechism,' says Canon Humfrey. 'They are not teaching error. Those doctrines Mrs McLeod is looking for are taught through *The Curriculum Directory* but they may not appear in a form in which they might have appeared pre-Vatican II. The bishops look at the theology of the RE programmes but they leave the methodology to the teachers and the advisors. Teaching methodology has changed and developed but the content stays the same.

'The short answer is that the main RE programmes are based on the Catechism through *The Curriculum Directory*, which is a summary of how the bishops want the Catechism to be taught in schools in England & Wales. Any religious education programme must show that it is implementing what *The Curriculum Directory* says.'

Mrs McLeod's views do appear a little extreme, for it seems highly unlikely that the bishops of England & Wales would deliberately try to water down the faith they were themselves ordained to preach. But there is no doubt that young Catholics are not taught the basics of their religion in a way their grandparents would recognize. While the method of teaching religion must change with the times, Mrs McLeod is not the only person who believes that the content has been radically altered too.

One Liverpool priest was so disturbed by the content of *Weaving the Web* that he risked the wrath of his archbishop to make a public stand against what he saw as a betrayal of Catholic children. Father Francis Marsden not only condemned it from his pulpit, he wrote a book that unequivocally condemned its use as a Catholic textbook.

'There were massive areas that were not covered at all or were misrepresented in some way,' he says. 'There were one or two pages on Mary and about six on Mohammed. If that's all the kids were going to get then they were going to end up with the idea that Mohammed was a much more important person.

'Given my situation in a fairly rough-and-tumble school on the outskirts of Liverpool, where the kids were fairly clueless, where the school was the only place where they would get very much of the teaching of Christianity, I thought it was disastrous. Moreover, I felt as a school chaplain that it was undermining what I was doing. When I first saw the books I felt more like leaving the priesthood than I've ever felt.'

Father Marsden discussed *Weaving the Web* – interestingly, the same title as a manual issued by a British coven of witches – with RE teachers in the school and discovered that it was compulsory throughout the Archdiocese of Liverpool. (In neighbouring Salford, Bishop Patrick Kelly had told his headteachers he didn't like it and didn't want it used.) So Father Marsden showed the book to his Sunday congregations, blaming it for their children's lack of knowledge of the Catholic faith. He received a standing ovation from Mass-goers – and a warning from Bishop John Rawsthorne, then an auxiliary in Liverpool, that he was not to speak on the subject again.

Father Marsden's response was simple. If he couldn't speak about *Weaving the Web* he would write about it. His essay, *Weaving A Web of Confusion*, was published by Parents' Concern in 1991. It was applauded by many but led to Father Marsden being summoned to explain himself to his Archbishop, the late Derek Worlock, who had personally endorsed the scheme for use throughout his archdiocese.

'The Archbishop wanted to shut me up,' says Father Marsden. 'I don't think he liked his scheme being criticized. But Archbishop Worlock had just written a pastoral letter talking about the importance of passing on the Faith and, at the same time, they had put out this scheme – and made it compulsory – where a lot of the faith was not present.'

It's not only *Weaving the Web* that has come under fire in recent years. In 1996 Cardinal Hume was forced to defend *The Bible for Children: The New Jerusalem version* against claims of pornography and calls for him to remove the imprimatur, the guarantee that it is free from doctrinal error. 'I do not believe the pictures are pornographic,' he said, 'no more than are many famous paintings and statues to be found in art galleries.'

The same year, complaints came flooding in about Clare Richards's book *Roman Catholic Christianity*, which, said its opponents, was far from Catholic in its views on contraception, the Trinity and the historicity of the Bible. Mrs Richards defended herself in the *Daily Telegraph*: 'I am teaching classes where half the Catholics have divorced parents and usually one girl has had an abortion. I cannot thump out the traditional Church teaching. It is not a devotional book, it is educational and it is not my position to be dogmatic.'

Bishop Peter Smith of East Anglia, in whose diocese the book had been granted its imprimatur, issued a statement saying the book was 'very well presented' but agreeing that there were 'some minor inaccuracies of fact'.

'However,' he added, 'a judgement that parts of the text suffer to a degree from inadequacy is not the same as judging them to be positively erroneous. The author is attempting to express the very profound teaching of the Church in language that will engage the pupils and help them to grow in their understanding of the fundamental mysteries of the faith.'

There was no doubt that some of the critics of *Roman Catholic Christianity* were quoting excerpts out of context but two years later, following a Vatican judgement that parts of the book were indeed not in accordance with Catholic teaching, Bishop Smith withdrew the book's imprimatur and ruled that it could no longer be used as a textbook in Catholic schools.

So just what do Catholic teenagers believe and what effect does 11 years of Catholic schooling have on them? The general feeling from the sixth form of St Mary's College, Wallasey, is: 'Catholicism is fine for those people who want to practise it. It's not for me but if that's what someone's into then that's OK.'

St Mary's is a 30-year-old co-educational voluntary-aided comprehensive in a pleasant suburb near the sea. A few years ago the school considered opting out of local authority control and becoming grant maintained. Despite pleas from the headteacher of the time, the parents made it clear that they wanted things to stay as they were.

The school has 1,250 pupils drawn from a wide range of social groupings. The catchment area includes large housing estates, leafy avenues and a pleasant seaside resort as well as industrial and brownfield sites. Parents belong to the middle and working classes and are fairly evenly represented in terms of job status or unemployment.

St Mary's is fed by five Catholic primaries and three school chaplains are often seen around the campus. The staff are committed to the school's Catholic ethos. When they are inducted, sixth-formers are reminded why the school exists and informed that they should subscribe to this ideal if they intend to stay there. The school's mission statement reminds pupils that 'inspired by the Spirit of Jesus Christ, our Catholic School Community is for the personal development of every member through service to each other'. Its aims are 'To encourage all to enjoy a personal relationship with God', 'To make prayer and worship part of everyday life' and 'To involve all members of the school community in prayer and worship'.

St Mary's sixth form are as friendly a bunch of youngsters as you could hope to meet. They are polite and welcoming to visitors and appear to treat each other and their teachers reasonably well. They are certainly 'Christian' in their approach to the poor, the marginalized and people with disabilities. But when it comes to things specifically Catholic, they seem hit by a bolt of total apathy. They're not anti-Catholic – it's just that they're not very pro-Catholic either.

A generation ago, a Catholic sixth form would have included a good smattering of practising Catholics – the God squad – and not a few cynics. Sixth form was a place where people bashed out religious, political and philosophical ideas. But the majority of the present sixth form at St Mary's, all of whom have come through the Catholic school system, hold generally neutral views on Catholicism.

From the group interviewed, 20 per cent said they went to Sunday Mass every week, although this figure is probably higher than the true percentage throughout the school. Just over half said they never went to Sunday Mass and the rest said they only entered a church for weddings, funerals or 'if my little sister's in a nativity play or something like that'.

Most said that their parents never went to Mass. Many of those who did attend regularly admitted it was because 'my mum would be upset if I didn't go', although one was involved in the parish music group and another said he went because 'of tradition and family guidance at first, but now because it provides a focus and it has served me well so far'.

The general feeling from the others was that Mass was 'boring'. 'I have heard it all before and don't need reminding,' said Anthony, while Steve has cottoned on to the age-old trick of popping his head into the church just long enough to collect the parish newsletter to prove to his mum that he's been. All Steve's family are practising Catholics but he also feels he's 'heard it all before' and might be more interested if priests could 'be given a free role and be more creative'. Ian pleaded the case for most of the computer game generation when he described Sunday Mass as 'repetitive, slow, no interaction'.

Quite a few of those who never went to Mass said they did 'have time for God' but Sunday morning was mostly reserved for sleeping and for part-time jobs. But it is interesting to note that in several cases, 'my mum and dad don't go any more so why should I?'

Most felt that a Catholic school like St Mary's was probably different from the neighbouring state schools, although they weren't quite sure why – apart from one who thought it offered 'a laughably biased opinion'. They pointed out the school's 'caring' attitude and its commitment to people with disabilities as an example.

The majority believed there was a difference between being married and just living with your partner, although only two people came anywhere near the concept of sacramental marriage by mentioning that wedding vows are taken before God.

'Marriage is a piece of paper,' said Tracy. 'It doesn't change how you feel about a partner. In some ways it causes more trouble because if you get divorced it turns into a big legal battle.' Jo added that 'if you make a promise to be faithful to your partner and live with them there is no real difference to being married'.

A third had no views on the rights and wrongs of sex outside marriage. The majority of those who did, thought it was all right and two thought it important that the people involved should actually care for each other. One said he felt 'a bit guilty after one-nighters' but was 'quite liberal' on the subject. 'You don't have to be married to someone to make love,' said Charlene, 'as long as you respect yourself and your partner.'

Again, a third of the group had no views on the Church's teaching on contraception. The others thought contraception not only desirable but positively virtuous as 'it doesn't just prevent pregnancy, it also prevents the spread of sexually transmitted diseases'. 'It's common sense,' said Chandler, 'and it helps to keep the population down.'

The few who thought homosexuality was wrong tended to be expounding homophobic views rather than the Church's teaching on the place of sex. The majority expressed a strong belief that banning gay sex was 'prejudice and discrimination' which was generally held to be contrary to Catholic belief.

'Gay couples should be allowed to have sex,' said Helen. 'I don't think there should be a big thing made of it as they cannot help their feeling. However, they should love the person they are having sex with.' And Louise added that 'just because their sexuality is different does not mean that they should be discriminated against'.

Three-quarters of the students couldn't understand why women can't be priests. Although a few were actually against women's ordination, only one of these could give any reason other than misogyny.

The majority thought priests should be free to marry, several pointing out that priests can't help falling in love. Only two of the students thought marriage would get in the way of priestly ministry. But the whole group was certainly appalled by tabloid stories of clergy scandals and there was a feeling that 'men like this who are trusted by whole communities' should be more strictly vetted. 'When you hear about priests doing things like abusing children it seems sick,' said Jenny. 'They are the people who are preaching God's words and when they let people down like that it destroys people's faith.'

Despite their own apathy, the students welcomed the increasing numbers of Catholics in Parliament. Most felt that both the House of Commons and the House of Lords should represent all the nation's beliefs, although one asked: 'How can you make non-Catholics live by laws that are affected by Catholic principles?'

The majority of the group were fond of their school and even those who never go near a church said they were happy to have had a church upbringing. 'I'm glad I was brought up with the Catholic religion,' said Stephanie. 'Perhaps the religion I was taught wasn't very strict but I feel I've been able to make my own choices without too much pressure.'

The St Mary's survey is far from scientific. It is a look at one single year group from one school out of 400 Catholic secondaries in England & Wales – the majority of which are comprehensives – and of course local traditions vary. But St Mary's is in a part of the country that has had a strong tradition of Mass-going over the last 100 years. If the views of St Mary's sixth form are in any way representative, then the current trend of emptying pews is far from over. It would appear churlish to blame Catholic secondary schools for not doing their job. If, at the age of 11, a youngster already comes from a non-practising family, there isn't much of a basis for secondary school teachers to work on. No matter how committed to their own faith and no matter how dedicated to the job of teaching – and the staff of St Mary's certainly appear committed – they cannot make the presumption that the majority of their pupils have even a basic grasp of the tenets of Catholicism. There's little they can do except start from scratch.

Daphne McLeod believes children remain uninspired because the current RE schemes are at best unimaginative and at worst full of error. 'By the time children get to 16 they have been in Catholic schools for 12 years and they have been consistently bored by the rubbish that's been put in front of them for RE. It's the most boring lesson on the curriculum when it should be the most interesting.

'The modern RE according to the books the bishops are promoting is pathetically silly. It teaches them as though they are a lot younger than they are. In history and science they are stretched but in RE they are treated like idiots and they pick that up very quickly. Just look at the books that are aimed at them.

'Imagine if they were maths teachers and all the way through primary school they had been taught rubbish, that two and two are five, everything wrong, then the best maths teacher in the world couldn't do senior maths with them. You have to unteach what they've learned to get it right.

'They've spent the whole of their primary school learning *Here I Am* or *Children of the Promise* – absolute idiotic rubbish – so when they come to senior school you can't start teaching them the Faith, you have to undo the harm that's been done and get it right.'

Whether or not the protests of Father Marsden and Mrs McLeod were heard, *Weaving the Web* has now fallen into disuse and a new secondary school scheme, *Icons*, should be available for autumn 2000 subject to final approval from the bishops. There have also been revisions of the primary school scheme, *Here I Am*.

'*Weaving the Web* was a resource for teachers,' explains Canon Humfrey. 'It wasn't a programme, or a textbook or the Catechism. It was a framework within which teachers would be enabled to teach coherently through the secondary phase. The bishops are very good at scrutinizing the documents that come out. All of them see all of the material before it's approved. They do take it seriously. Every bishop has seen every page of the *Icons* material. Revisions were made and the bishops have seen the revised version.

'*Here I Am* and *Icons* are part of a national project which has been running for some years, initiated and promoted by the Bishops' Conference. They are looked at and approved by the Bishops' Conference. There is no other RE programme which has that authenticity. While anybody else can write a programme, providing it's based on *The Curriculum Directory*, it wouldn't have the calibre and the quality of a national programme which has been through this long consultation process.'

Mick Brown, Head of RE at St Mary's College, is defensive about primary school catechetical programmes. A father of four, he recently witnessed his eldest child making his first Communion and was impressed by the course that led up to it.

'My lad made his first holy Communion last year and he knew there was something special about it,' says Mick. 'He knew he was receiving Jesus in the Eucharist for the first time. Intellectually he accepted that. They have a whole year of celebration in Year 3 in primary school and they do prepare them very, very well from what I can see.

'I think the approach of *Here I Am* is very good, it's very strong. They've actually produced something that takes you through Catholic doctrine. So it is covered, but not in the traditional sense. It's trying to start from the kids' experience and taking them to a position where they might be able to understand it. But you don't get a faith to live by. You get a series of teachings that have no relevance in their lives. This is the bridge that we have to make in secondary schools. The faith isn't just a given faith, it's a faith that makes sense in their lives. If we can't make the faith make sense in their lives then we're wasting our time. And I believe we can.'

He says that he and his staff cannot presume that youngsters coming to St Mary's College at the age of 11 have any tradition of practice of their religion other than what they have been taught in primary school. 'The grounding that was traditionally there isn't there any more. You can presume nothing apart from what they have been taught in the primary school itself. A lot of parents aren't practising and therefore a lot of the kids aren't practising, and what you are trying to do is alien to them.'

Mr Brown, who describes himself as 'a fully paid up member' of the Catholic Church, and who is obviously committed to both his faith and his job, believes that national syllabuses are necessary but he is also optimistic that the current 'exciting' debate about religious education in schools will lead the whole Church into a rediscovery of what it actually believes. 'What we're talking about in RE is what the Church should be asking itself. We have to go back to Jesus and see where he started. But we don't. We go straight to tradition and dogma and teaching and we miss out a huge chunk there.

'The whole Jesus thing is of the Incarnation, of God becoming human. As soon as you start stressing divinity and talking divinity – that's what happened in the first 300 years – you have to go back and start asking yourself some real questions about what do we mean by that, what do we mean by the words that we use?

'If you talk about transubstantiation, if you talk about salvation, what are you trying to get at that the kids can make sense and meaning of? It means asking ourselves, before we get to the kids, some fundamental questions. I think the whole process of that is really exciting.'

Less than five miles away from St Mary's is St Anselm's College, a Christian Brothers foundation. St Anselm's, like many other religious schools of that time, once had a reputation for literally putting the fear of God – and fear of the occasional strapping – into pupils.

These days the school has a lay head, Chris Cleugh, who says that, while he believes his pupils' regular Mass attendance is slightly higher than that of St Mary's, it wouldn't be anywhere near as high as a generation ago. Mr Cleugh's predecessors would have drummed into their young charges that missing Sunday Mass was a mortal sin and would have thought nothing of asking who had and hadn't been to church that week.

'I couldn't do that now, nor would I want to,' says Mr Cleugh. 'The only way you can do it is by example and that is what we try to do. How do you define a Catholic? Is a Catholic a piece of paper that says you were baptized? Or is a Catholic somebody who can produce a piece of paper to prove that they go to Mass each week? I'm very sad but in this day and age there are relatively few in the last category.'

St Anselm's has exactly the same problems as St Mary's. Many pupils come from nominally Catholic families who do not practise their religion. This makes the job of Catholic schools an uphill struggle but Mr Cleugh rebuts the idea that Catholic schools are to blame for the lack of interest among Catholic teenagers. 'I don't think that's in any way fair. The schools do a good job in a secular world. You have to appreciate where the student's coming from. If there's no practice in the home then there's not going to be practice just because there's practice in school.'

Father Francis Marsden is quite sympathetic to claims from the St Mary's College teenagers that Mass is 'boring'. He blames the quick-thrill attitude of contemporary society where even TV programmes are broken up by advertisements into digestible chunks. But he believes that, within certain parameters, parish priests can make Sunday Mass more appealing to the quick-thrill generation.

'I was taught what the Mass really is and I was still a bit bored,' he says. 'At that age you're not very amenable. The other side is that our society is one of blatant entertainment and immediate satisfaction. I think it is very difficult for young people brought up in that society because they cannot actually concentrate.

'You're a bit stuck with the liturgy. It has to appeal to all ages. If you focus it too much on the 14-year-olds then you lose the 74-year-olds. A parish priest on a Sunday morning is in a very difficult position because he's trying to provide a balance. He's also got what the Church has given him, what's laid down in the rubrics and it's not really up to him to alternate.

'We tend to regard what's in the Missal as everything though, in fact, that is a basis to be inculturated. That's the minimum, if you like. How we then embellish that with songs and music and procession is left up to us. In Africa Mass can go on for two hours with music and dancing. Over here we've gone the other way, we've destroyed our inculturation, what we had up to the sixties.'

Father Richard Moroney might have met the challenge head on when he confronted the parents of his first Communion children but, like Mick Brown and Chris Cleugh, he doesn't believe the primary schools or the religious education programmes can be blamed for either the children's ignorance or the parents' lethargy. 'I don't think it's a question of blame, it's just how things have developed. The Church teaches the same as it's always taught with regard to the sacraments. As soon as you apportion blame you are condemning somebody and I don't think anybody is to be condemned. We know what's necessary.

'We have to start off from where we are and what we have is not such a bad situation, it's just a different situation. We deal with this different situation in the best way we can – not by compromising the Faith, not by getting depressed about it, but by acknowledging that people have a choice.

'Parents need to be honest. They must not get their children baptized unless they can bring them up in the practice of the Faith. I think that God can only work through the honest person, through the honest non-believer. The person who's pulling the wool over their own eyes also separates themselves a great distance from God because they're not seeking the truth, they're seeking the best for the family and themselves, perhaps to get their children into Catholic schools. And this is not, at the end of the day, what faith is about.'

Similarly, Archbishop Cormac understands the complaints of young people. In 1983, he issued a pastoral letter calling on parishes and deaneries 'to give opportunities to our younger parishioners to discover the presence of Christ in their lives'. He said that when young people describe their experience of the Church as 'boring and unjoyful' they mean 'the lack of a sense of community and the lack of welcome that they experience on Sunday at Mass':

> Young people need to have a place where they can discover faith and spend time with Jesus. This may be in school, or at home, at Mass on Sunday, or more likely at a youth event where they can share together in an atmosphere of acceptance and joy, some of the aspirations of their faith.
>
> Young people find it puzzling and confusing to live out the demands of Christ in today's world. Many of them, for example, find it difficult to accept the traditional views on sexual morality. It should be remembered that Christian teaching will often clash with the 'common sense' of the world.

He went on to remind parents, and the whole Catholic community, that instead of grumbling about the lack of practice among young people, they should be leading by example:

Young people today are impressed by deeds and not by words. Frankly, a big obstacle to them today is not intellectual doubt in Christianity, but rather the un-Christian lifestyle of many of us who think we are good Christians. How little, sometimes, do we live out in our lives what we proclaim with our lips.

The RE schemes currently being piloted and published could be in use by September 2000 and only time will tell exactly what fruit they will bear. But they cannot be made scapegoats for the problems of passing on the Catholic faith to the next generation, a task that belongs to the whole Catholic community. As Archbishop Cormac has already said, 'we have to find new ways of reaching out to people, especially young people, in our society today and that's not easy'.

✦

4. Everlasting Love

In 1996 Archbishop Cormac published a pastoral letter in which he compared marriage to those indissoluble partnerships of Laurel and Hardy and Torvill and Dean. There are plenty of married couples around who might see their relationship as more akin to Punch and Judy, but on the whole, the institution of marriage has served society well for thousands of years. He wrote:

> You don't form a partnership for its own sake. You do so in order to create something else. People live and work together because they want to achieve something that can only be best done when done together. People get married not just to do what 'I want to do' but in order to do 'what we want to do', namely to make a home, bring up a family, share each other's gifts. Partners operate as a unity and can do far more than one person.

As far back as 1945 the critic and writer Cyril Connolly said that 'the tragedy of modern marriage is that married couples no longer enjoy the support of society, although marriage, difficult at any time, requires every social sanction'. The Second World War had caused huge social change, and divorce – which had become more acceptable since the 1936 Abdication crisis – was now becoming common. Couples who had married at the outbreak of war, and had then been separated for four or five years, discovered that it was difficult to take up where they had left off.

More than half a century later Cyril Connolly would perhaps not be surprised to discover that up to one-third of all marriages now end in divorce. If you add in the many partnerships that are not recognized by Church or State, it would appear that the majority of Britons are either no longer capable of sustaining a long-term relationship or simply don't want to. Of course, you can reverse the figures and see that two-thirds of marriages *are* for life. That still means there are more than 150,000 divorces every year in England & Wales and up to 300,000 people have found their lives turned upside down, to say nothing of the heartache caused to any children who may be involved.

For Catholics, divorce can involve far more than a legal wrangle and emotional upset. Having made vows before God, in the presence of one of his ministers and the local church community, a practising Catholic really will expect to live that commitment for life, even if their partner doesn't have the stamina to last the course.

'I am still married,' says Rita, whose husband left her ten years ago and divorced her two years later. 'I made those vows for life and I meant them. I'm still living in the family home and the children still come back here, return to the nest if you like.

'We are both Catholics. We met at the parish youth club and were engaged for nearly two years before we walked down the aisle. We were both 25 then, old enough to know what we were doing. We had a nuptial Mass with all our family and our friends from the parish and both our priests came to the reception. That really was a Catholic wedding.

'All the children were baptized in the same church and went to the parish school. We were one of those families who took up a whole row at Sunday Mass. Both me and [her husband] were involved in all the parish groups – the choir, the SVP, all that sort of thing.

'When he left I couldn't get my head round it. Even when the divorce papers came through I didn't take them seriously. They were just bits of paper with a stamp on them. I still had my marriage certificate saying I'd been married in church.

'Everyone in the parish has been great, very caring, it's that sort of parish. But I still feel a bit out of things. I see all these married couples I've known since we were all in the Young Mums group together 30 years ago. They still invite me to parish socials or round for dinner but I feel incomplete somehow. If I was a widow it might be easier but I'm not. My husband is with another woman.

'I couldn't imagine ever marrying someone else while [my husband] is still alive. As far as I'm concerned I'm still married in the eyes of God and the Church.'

Divorce is not easy. It is one of the most traumatic events we can ever experience. It can lead to stress and trigger mental illness. But still we allow people to get married in apparent haste. Tell your bishop you want to be a priest and you can expect months of discernment before you get anywhere near a seminary and years of training before you are ordained. Enter a convent or a monastery and you are embarking on a long process of formation and temporary vows before you make the final commitment. But announce your plans to be married and you can be standing in a church, surrounded by large hats, making lifelong vows before God within a matter of weeks.

While a civil divorce can be obtained in less than six months there is no equivalent within the Catholic Church. The only way a Catholic can be declared free to marry again is if their first marriage was null and void in the first place. Up to 2,000 Catholics petition for an annulment every year. Half of these cases are withdrawn before they are completed and, of those remaining, about 90 per cent are deemed not to have been valid marriages in the first place. But, because the Church takes marriage very seriously, the process is far from painless.

Being divorced and remarried is 'the unforgivable sin', claims Wendy Bailey, a 50-year-old development worker with an international aid agency, who returned to the Church after an absence of more than 20 years. During that time her first marriage had ended after only 18 months and she had married Peter, her present husband.

'I, like many other people, thought I couldn't have an annulment because I had children. I didn't know the grounds for annulment at all.'

However, Wendy soon discovered that an annulment was necessary if she was to return to receiving the sacraments and so she embarked upon what would be a two-year process.

'Going to the tribunal was traumatic,' she recalls. 'It's a fairly direct route but I was so stressed I seemed to get lost. The priest was very gentle. We sat face to face and he wrote down everything I said. He asked me questions, which helped. He asked about how we had prepared for my first marriage. After half an hour I had a terrible nosebleed, which I've never had in my life, and it was simply the amazing stress of going over all that pain.

'The priest said we should go forward to find witnesses who knew me before the marriage. It's not about trying to find blame, it's about trying to find grounds within Church law that say you did not understand what it was you were doing. And I didn't. There are people who go out to interview the witnesses, not always priests. They travel all over the country to talk to people, that's the lengths they go to. I had to approach my ex-husband and he didn't want anything to do with it.

'My first marriage was very painful to go over. But as soon as I'd finished talking about it, I felt that it was beginning to heal. I had always felt very guilty about the end of the marriage. I felt I was obviously such a horrible person that I provoked the situation, so I took the blame for it.'

Having just returned to the Church, through contact with a priest she describes as 'wonderful', Wendy was devastated to learn that she could not receive Communion until her annulment was granted. 'That was the hardest part. Because I had just come back to the Church and it meant so much. What was worse to contemplate was supposing I didn't get the annulment. What would happen to me then? Would I be forever excluded?'

Despite feeling that she was 'in limbo', Wendy threw herself into the round of parish activity, becoming involved in fundraising, singing in the choir and representing the

Association of Divorced Catholics (ASDC) on the parish council. 'When I joined ASDC and became very active in it, I felt I had to trumpet it and pronounce it and make it an acceptable part of the parish. It's a lot of like-minded people going through the same traumas who understand your pain, who are not judgemental and who can support each other.'

To the casual observer, the decision on who can and who cannot obtain an annulment can appear quite arbitrary. In fact, every case is judged on its own merits by a tribunal of skilled Church lawyers, both clerical and lay. They spend up to two years considering whether the couple concerned were in a position to make their wedding vows freely and to give their consent to a serious lifelong commitment. But there have been questionable cases when European aristocrats and royalty have been granted their annulment in a comparatively short time to allow State business to continue unhindered.

Margaret Philips says she is embarrassed by the annulment of her son's marriage. The 50-year-old mother of four is convinced the request was only granted because the family has a relative who is a priest with a good knowledge of canon law.

'They had been married for 11 years and had two children,' says Mrs Philips, who became a Catholic when she married nearly 30 years ago. 'I really don't see how the Church can now say that marriage never existed. I have friends in the parish whose children's marriages lasted only a matter of months with no offspring and they have been repeatedly turned down in their requests for an annulment.'

Similarly, 'Kath' has refused to apply for an annulment, despite being advised by her parish priest that she could be successful. 'It's complete rubbish,' she says. 'We were married for more than 30 years. We had two children and we have four grandchildren. My husband left me for another woman. But, with the best will in the world, you can't pretend that marriage never existed. That's what an annulment is, a decree saying there was no marriage in the first place. Yes, it fell apart and, yes, I wish there was some way I could now be free to marry if I wanted to, but I won't admit there was no marriage there in the first place.

That's like saying that more than half my life just didn't exist. I'm a granny now so I have proof that it did.'

Wendy Bailey explains that, like a lot of people, Kath doesn't really understand what annulment is all about. 'It's not saying the marriage didn't happen. It's saying it should never have been. It's not saying it wasn't a real marriage. It's saying that, with hindsight, that marriage shouldn't have taken place because the circumstances weren't right at the beginning. I think a lot more people could try for an annulment if they knew about it – because it's not well publicized – and if they were encouraged to do so. Once you get into the process it's very fair.'

Although the Church's rules on marriage can appear a minefield, they were created to put a stop to earlier, more cruel, divorce laws, according to Father John Redford, director of distance learning at the Maryvale Institute in Birmingham.

'Jesus's teaching regarding divorce was totally revolutionary both with regard to Old Testament law and with regard to Roman law,' he explains. 'Divorce in the ancient world happened not by decree of court, as in our day, but simply by a man – the bread-winner – throwing his wife out of the house, often on to the street to beg or to starve.

'The law of Moses stipulated that the man had to have a reason for putting his wife out of the house and marrying another and the rabbis in Jesus's day differed as to the gravity of this reason. In St Matthew's Gospel Jesus says that divorce itself was only allowed by God because of the hardness of people's hearts but that, from creation, it was not always so. God made male and female to become one body. No more then would people separate from their own bodies than separate from their spouses, two in one flesh. And there is no case when a man may divorce his wife and marry another.

'But did Jesus mean this as a law? Is what he said about marriage presenting an ideal to be realized, but now a law to be formulated by the canon lawyers of successive generations? Many Christians today would argue in this way from the words of Jesus about divorce. However, it seems to me, the words of

Jesus about divorce only make sense precisely as the basis of a specific and concrete law.

'The challenge today is quite simple. We cannot in any way reduce the force of Jesus's words. He means precisely what he says, that the marriage bond among his disciples is absolute.'

Sheilagh Preston, national president of the Union of Catholic Mothers (UCM), believes it is important that the parish community is understanding of people having marriage problems, whether they are remarried or not.

'Marriages do sometimes go wrong and we need to have compassion,' she says. 'I know a number of people who have been divorced and remarried and who have suffered a great deal because of the lack of sacraments, and I personally have a great deal of sympathy towards them. The fact that some of us are in stable marriages doesn't mean that we don't appreciate those that aren't. With the best will in the world things do go wrong. I don't condemn anyone, because there but for the grace of God go any one of us. In the past we haven't been as compassionate as we might.'

Father John Daley, parish priest of St Teresa, Birstall, Leicester, says parishioners should welcome those in difficult marital situations with kindness and love. 'You have to handle the parish gossips in your own way. A genuinely concerned person will understand the Church wants kindness, it wants love and it wants right to be done.

'There are two clear theologies in the Church, moral theology and pastoral theology. Canon law sets down the conditions of marriage and remarriage. Moral theology sets out to say what is clearly right and wrong. Pastoral theology starts from the fact that no one is ever outside the love of God, without forgetting the other theology.

'Supposing you are in a relationship that is hopelessly wrong morally, pastorally we can work together because all you need is the intention to work towards the fullness of God's love. The ideal moment will come in a person's life when morally and pastorally it is all right. But you have to start where someone is.'

Father Daley explains that in some circumstances a priest will bless the two people involved even though he can't bless their relationship. 'In difficult situations the Church will always bless people,' he says. 'Even if it can't bless the union as sacramental, it can bless the people. This is why some of our men will bless homosexual couples, perhaps not happily, but they won't refuse, on the grounds that they can't refuse God's blessing to anyone. But they make it clear they are not blessing the union. Sometimes this will help a couple enough to give the Catholic partner the sense of still belonging to the Church. They may not be able to come to the sacraments because their marriage is outside the Church, but their life isn't.'

Priests like Father Daley cannot, in these circumstances, tell someone they are free to receive Communion. On the other hand they cannot refuse anyone who approaches the altar, because they cannot presume to know the exact situation.

'If I were to give away at the altar that someone was not in good standing whom everybody thought was, I would be wrong under the Church's law,' explains Father Daley. 'Who knows what happened the previous day? Who knows what sacramental resolution of someone's lifestyle or problem has been granted? You do not know. For a priest to presume that they know someone's situation at the altar is a defamation of character by judgement and you cannot make it. You do not know the state of grace of the individual person and so you presume. The only time you can refuse Communion is when you know it's a set-up.'

Contrary to popular belief, Catholics who have divorced are not barred from receiving Communion. The problem only arises if they remarry and are therefore, technically, committing adultery. Father Francis Marsden, described by parishioners as 'a lion in the pulpit and a lamb in the confessional' takes a fairly strict view on what he describes as this 'painful' predicament.

'Ultimately it comes to the genital question,' he says. 'If a remarried couple can live as brother and sister then they can go back to the sacraments. It's a direct choice between sex and holy Communion. The divorced remarried have that problem and there are many painful situations.'

Father Richard Moroney puts it rather more gently, saying he would invite remarried people 'to get to know who Jesus Christ is'.

'That's all that God became man for,' he says, 'so you can get to know him. The Church is the vehicle for introducing people to the person of Christ. Jesus didn't come to destroy the laws of the prophets, he came to fulfil them, to go further than them. So much of our Catholicism has been a rule book without Christ. It's just an institution without any spirit, so that's all that people see. I would say that Jesus came to take away our sins and shame. You hear about things like the Catholic guilt complex. Where's that come from? It hasn't come from Jesus.'

His words ring true for Wendy Bailey, who, having been told she could not receive Communion during the annulment process, felt excluded when everyone else left their seats to process to the altar. 'When I was a youngster it wasn't everyone who went to Communion. But now everybody goes, so people like me are the people you step over in the bench and you wonder why they don't go to Communion. Technically I was fornicating, living in sin with my own husband. What kind of impression does that leave you with? I don't believe that I was living in sin for 13 years.

'There's such a mixed reaction from priests. In the ASDC we had lots of people who needed help and we had wonderful pastors who would help, who were so sympathetic and understanding. Some had indicated to me that they would give me Communion but I wouldn't receive it. Because I did agree with the Church, painful as it was.'

In Wendy's case the story had a happy ending. After two years her annulment was granted and she and Peter were remarried in a Catholic church. 'When the annulment came through, when the letter came through the door, I did not want to open it. The relief was incredible and the joy of going to Communion for the first time was beyond belief. I still feel huge compassion for everyone left behind.'

But there was a bitter twist when Wendy's priest said the wedding should take place in the convent chapel rather than in the parish church as he wanted to avoid any scandal.

'I really didn't agree with that,' says Wendy. 'I thought that was wrong. It should be a huge celebration of the prodigal son coming back. How can it be a scandal? We're all sinners.'

For many Catholics the image of the Holy Family of Jesus, Mary and Joseph remains an ideal. And for many older British Catholics that ideal was reinforced by Pathé newsreels of the Royal Family of King George VI, Queen Elizabeth and Princesses Elizabeth and Margaret. More recent events leading to the divorces of three of the Queen's children and her sister show that divorce can happen 'even in the best of families'. Or, more realistically, the breakdown of marriages and the ensuing break-up of the family unit is an increasingly everyday fact of life. Even so, the Church relies heavily on the imagery of bride and groom or husband and wife. Many parish activities are designed with family groups in mind and Catholic societies are often at the forefront of campaigning for laws to support or protect the ideal of the family. Much of this can be painful for those living in what are so quaintly called 'irregular unions'.

When, in 1995, the Government announced plans to reform the Divorce Act and speed up the civil divorce procedure, the bishops of England & Wales published a statement stressing that marriage was 'raised by Christ the Lord to the dignity of sacrament' and was 'absolutely essential to the well-being of society'. The bishops continued:

> All marriages, not only marriages between Christians, need to incorporate certain values, amongst which are unconditional love and respect between spouses and especially for the children, faithfulness to promises solemnly and publicly made and the willingness to enter into the process of reconciliation when the relationship gets into difficulties and hurt is inflicted.

The following January Cardinal Hume reminded Parliament that it was handling 'a moral, social and political project of immense proportions' and called for an extension to the proposed 12-month waiting period. Writing in *The Tablet*, he said a 'no-fault' divorce would send out 'a moral message that marriage is a temporary relationship which exists principally for the fulfilment of the individual spouses'.

The bishops were again forced to speak out in support of marriage when, in November 1998, Home Secretary Jack Straw presented a consultation on 'supporting families' that proposed prenuptial agreements to ease the pain of marriage break-up.

'There is much to applaud in this document,' said Bishop Peter Smith of East Anglia, 'although there are certain aspects about which we have reservations. We wholeheartedly welcome the publication of a document with such an emphasis on supporting families. Families are at the core of our communities and our nation and it is excellent that they are being given the significance which they deserve. However, written prenuptial agreements seem to imply an expectation of marriage breakdown and undermine the notion of total commitment to marriage.'

There was, therefore, a collective sigh of relief when, in September 1999, Education Secretary David Blunkett announced that children would be taught about the importance of marriage as part of the new schools curriculum. For Catholic women's groups this was a particular victory. The Catholic Women's League (CWL) and the Union of Catholic Mothers had been campaigning for such a move for some time and had presented a 42,000-signature petition to Downing Street the previous July.

'We were very pleased they listened to us,' said CWL national president Anne Fox. 'Marriage is a standard and it is a base to build on. Children need that security. They need to have the father and the mother there and they have to be together. They prove that they want to take the step by making the vows of marriage. It is an ideal and we don't live in an ideal world, but it is something we should aspire to.

'The legal world has made it difficult for marriage. It's too easy now to get out of these things and people don't want to work at it. But there's not enough preparation for the state of marriage and the responsibilities that go with it.'

Bishop Vincent Nichols joined forces with Alan Chesters, Anglican Bishop of Blackburn, to welcome the curriculum, which, they stated, should play a part in promoting 'pupils' spiritual, moral, social and cultural development and, in particular, developing principles for distinguishing between right and wrong'. They continued:

> This should send a clear signal to schools in an age when, too often, morality is seen as just a matter of opinion. It is very encouraging to see the Government demonstrate this resolve when there is such widespread anxiety about the influences – particularly through the media and advertising – shaping the attitudes of many young people and frequently encouraging sexual activity without responsibility.
>
> We must address the deep moral confusion in our society and be unafraid to name the ideals and principles which serve long-term stability in marriage and thereby offer the best environment for the raising of children.

Bishops Nichols and Chesters summed up, however, by stressing that 'Schools can only be expected to do so much. The responsibility lies with all of us, and particularly with parents. We each have responsibility for the example we set by how we live.'

The bishops' view has the unequivocal support of the Association of Catholic Women. Chairman Josephine Robinson stresses that 'marriage is absolutely of the social and religious essence'.

'The relationship between a man and a woman in marriage provides commitment,' she says. 'It has to be unlimited both in time and generosity. Children need stability. Just imagine, Mum goes off in the middle and the child thinks not only "I am unloved by Mum", but therefore "I must be unlovable". And if a child has a feeling that he or she is unlovable, it's not surprising that their behaviour becomes disruptive and that anxieties appear. For so long people have said that children are resilient and they get over it. To some extent, thank God, that's true but it's not wholly true.'

Mrs Robinson believes that preparation for marriage can begin both by example in the home and in sex education in school. 'We should certainly prepare children more fully. The whole of sex education should be taught on the basis of the theology of the body, that is to say that the body has been given by God, it has specific functions, it is a very precious thing and therefore must not be misused in all sorts of different ways. What it is growing to is this business of relationships which, for most people, is marriage.'

Despite being a happily married wife and mother, Mrs Robinson feels the parish community can help single people who may feel excluded from the many family-based activities in Church life. 'I think it's hard for unmarried people, especially unmarried women, who feel that because of the Church's emphasis on marriage and the family they are a bit out of it. The answer in the parish is every possible inclusivity. If the parish is a place of faith and prayer there should be a feeling that we're all there together because we have a close bond through our faith.

'I can think of no better institution to provide this sense of community than the Catholic Church because everybody, whatever their station or age or level of education, has something absolutely fundamental to their life which is shared by a whole lot of other people who come together at least once a week.'

Despite claims of the breakdown of marriage and family life, UCM president Sheilagh Preston insists she is an 'optimist' and is keen to point out that 'there are marriages that are sticking together through thick and thin'. She blames the media, and magazines in particular, for presenting 'sex as the most important thing in the world', and something that can be enjoyed out of commitment. 'Sex *is* very important,' she says, 'but it's not the most important thing in a marriage. There has to be a lot of give and take.'

Despite the UCM's commitment 'to uphold the sanctity, responsibilities and permanence of marriage and family life', Mrs Preston says it is important that the parish community should accept and support people whose marriages have broken down. 'The ideal isn't always possible and we have to accept that.

As mothers we know from our own families that it doesn't always work out, yet our children and our grandchildren are just as sacred to us. We have members whose marriages have broken down and there is no problem with that. We hope the UCM will accept them with the same kindness and tolerance with which we hope they will accept anybody. We are very compassionate. We have a very loving fellowship and that's something we need to spell out a bit more. The days when people were ostracized are long since gone.

'If you come to one of our conferences you will go away feeling the love and warmth that people have for one another. That's one of the things we forget in this world. If you read the papers we're all fighting and knocking each other about, but there is still a great deal of love and a great deal of compassion about.'

Given his own large, and extended, family, Archbishop Cormac should know a thing or two about family life. Even so – or perhaps as a result – he has called for more support for marriage and the family within both the Church and the wider community:

> It seems to me that there is a cultural onslaught against the family in our society which increasingly undermines stability and the healthy upbringing of children. I pray that there will be a renewed commitment to support the family so that today, even amidst so many difficulties, the family will remain the guardian and sanctuary of life.

Even so, Father Paul Jennings, who heads the marriage tribunal in Arundel & Brighton diocese, stresses that Archbishop Cormac takes a very pastoral and caring approach to people who find themselves in marriage difficulties. 'Archbishop Cormac is very, very understanding,' he says. 'He certainly sees from where people are coming but at the same time he is a man of the Church. So he tries to do everything he can to balance the teaching of the Church, and the Church's understanding of marriage, with the pastoral needs of the people entrusted to his care. He has always done everything he can to balance the two.'

'Whenever people have gone directly to him he has always treated them with great care and pastoral concern. He has never disregarded them. He is very conscious of the situation people find themselves in and he is also very conscious of the way the Church can help them.'

As Archbishop Cormac himself said, the day before his installation as tenth Archbishop of Westminster:

When you look around and see so many broken marriages and one-parent families, your heart goes out to these people who have very, very hard lives. We are not condemning them – that would be entirely wrong. The key point is how do you recognize the compassion, the brokenness, but at the same time uphold and say what is true in terms of marital relationship. It is quite a mission for the Church to speak with the right tone.

✝

5. Is There An Enemy Within?

In March 1994 the Anglican Bishop of Bristol, Barry Rogerson, ordained 32 women to the priesthood. Outside Bristol Cathedral, Catholic campaigners for women's ordination carried banners declaring 'Equal Rites! RC Women Next!' and 'Women Priests Yes! Misogynists No!' Inside, Father Mark Cornelis, a Belgian priest, made the unscheduled prayer that 'the Roman Catholic Church may finally be able to overcome ossified and discriminating legislation, and allow women to be ordained and lead the way in preaching God's word, in celebrating the Eucharist, and in showing ways for the community of faith to go'.

Writing in *The Universe* newspaper at the time, Archbishop Cormac explained the difficulties arising from the Church of England's decision to admit women to ordained ministry:

> Clearly the decision of the General Synod in 1992 to admit women to the priesthood has had considerable repercussions throughout the Church. It is very important to understand that the basic question is not about whether or not women can be ordained but about the authority of the Church of England to make such a decision. For those Anglicans who see the Church of England as an integral part of the Catholic Church, this is the key question.

Three weeks after the Bristol ordinations, Pope John Paul sent a letter to the world's bishops saying that Catholic women could become altar servers for the first time. The announcement was welcomed by some of those who backed women's ordination as a step in the right direction. But the difference was palpable – Anglican women could *become* priests but Catholic women could only *serve* priests.

Pope John Paul had made it clear that the ordination of women to the priesthood in the Church of England caused 'a most serious obstacle to any hope of union between the Catholic Church and the Anglican Communion'. Further, he forbade any more discussion on the subject.

The debate over the rights and wrongs of women priests has raged for decades. Ordination aside, there's no doubt that women were seen almost as a different species for many centuries. St Paul ordered that women should keep quiet in church and that their heads should be covered. The 1913 edition of *The Catholic Encyclopaedia* even goes so far as to state that 'the female sex is in some respects inferior to the male sex, both as regards body and soul', although it does concede that 'woman's work is in itself of equal value with that of a man, as the work performed by both is ennobled by the same human dignity'. But with a few obvious exceptions – St Hilda ran a double monastery and presided over the Synod of Whitby and St Clare was the only woman religious to have written her own rule – the men were the ringmasters in the great big top of the Church, while the women swept up the sawdust.

Throughout the 20th century there have been more women than men in our pews. But it was the men and boys who were altar servers and led the annual Blessed Sacrament Procession. In some churches, even taking the weekly collection was seen as a specifically male occupation. Once back home Catholic wives could still not expect equality with their spouses. Pope Leo XIII had ruled that 'The husband is ruler of the family and the head of the wife. The woman is to be subordinate and obedient to the husband. The husband ruling represents the image of Christ and the wife obedient the image of the Church'.

Right up to the 1960s women were only allowed to pass through the gate in the altar rails for two reasons: to get married or to scrub the sanctuary steps. At one time they were not even allowed to sing in the choir if the choir stalls were located beyond the communion rail. Pope Pius X went so far as to legislate that 'singers in the church have a real liturgical office and that, therefore, woman as being incapable of exercising such office, cannot be admitted to form part of the choir or of the musical chapel'. As late as the 1960s the bishops' music commission stated that women might only sing in the choir if there were no boys available, and even then they were not allowed to wear liturgical robes. Clifton Cathedral was one of the first major Catholic institutions to dispense with the tradition and install a mixed – and robed – choir when it opened in 1973. As Aunt Kate complains in James Joyce's *The Dead*:

> I know all about the honour of God, but I think it's not at all honourable for the people to turn the women out of the choirs that have slaved there all their lives and put whipper-snappers of boys over their heads. I suppose it is for the good of the Church, if the Pope does it, but there's such a thing as common everyday politeness and gratitude.

With the advent of lay readers, women were eventually allowed to read publicly from the Old Testament and the Epistles – the Gospel is reserved for someone who has been ordained deacon, by definition a man. And once eucharistic ministers were instituted, there were far more women willing and able to be commissioned than men. Take a look around the average Catholic church and it soon becomes obvious that it is mostly women, usually older women, who are entrusted with the job of taking Communion to the sick of the parish.

Outside the liturgy it is the women of the parish who raise money, visit the sick, cook for the clergy, turn up for parish meetings and do the thousand and one jobs that keep the local church ticking over. On a national level women hold posts within the

Bishops' Conference and head committees and commissions that make major decisions on Church life. As more than one cleric has commented, 'We can't have women priests – there has to be something left for men to do.'

Looking simply at the gender of the people in the pew the Catholic Church appears to be matriarchal. But according to a report published in 1983, women suffer sexual discrimination in a male-dominated Church. The report from a working party of the Laity Commission, an advisory body of the Bishops' Conference, took the unfortunate title of *Why Can't A Woman Be More Like A Man* – unfortunate because it is a quotation from *My Fair Lady* and an extremely misogynistic number sung by confirmed bachelor Professor Henry Higgins.

The Commission looked at issues that were 'likely to generate emotional rather than rational discussion', and that would reflect 'what people really felt and believed, as opposed to what they considered to be the appropriate and orthodox response'. In other words the whole thing was in Churchspeak and inaccessible to those who didn't hold a basic degree in rhetoric.

The report claimed that women wanted, above all, to serve the Church but constantly felt pushed into traditional roles and that clergy patronized them and kept them at a distance. The women surveyed thought the Church was 'authoritarian and hard, unfeeling and lacking in compassion, more interested in upholding "truth" and "right" than in the fallible human beings whom it bruises in the process'. Thankfully they still had 'a love and understanding of the Church which enabled the women to talk about their feelings without bitterness and anger'.

Ouch! But the national secular press loved it. 'RC women protest', said the *Guardian*. 'Catholic women offended by sexism', said the *Morning Star*. And, from the *Daily Telegraph*, a particular favourite: 'The tea and buns brigade drop a religious bombshell'.

It was certainly a 'bombshell' for many women in the pew who had absolutely no idea that they were being oppressed in the first place.

'It's absolute rubbish, of course,' says Josephine Robinson, chairman of the Association of Catholic Women, which was set up in the late 1980s as a direct counterblast to the feminist movement in the Church. 'This sort of thing is so absurd and so misleading and gets the Church terrible publicity.

'However, I think the worst of the threat of the dotty religious feminism is over. It's more worrying now that they have filtered down. These feminist theologians are horribly influential in all sorts of academic corners both here and in America. Their ideas percolate down, which can be very damaging for young people who are taught by them in schools. Women who have studied theology formally do tend to be rather feminist in tone.'

And Anne Fox, national president of the Catholic Women's League, says she has definitely never felt oppressed. 'In some instances women have been ignored when it comes to decision-making within the Church. But on the other hand, times are changing. We are getting more and more involved and our opinions are being sought now. The clergy themselves are changing and the young priests coming out now see things very differently.

'We are the people who are doing the work. If you were to empty the Church of women next Sunday, it would be closed the following Sunday because more women than men go to church. If you think about the work that's done within the Church, I think you can count the percentage of men on one hand compared with the women. But that's traditional, it's nothing new.

'We have a lot to offer the Church which has perhaps not been sufficiently recognized. But I don't have a problem with equality of the sexes. I think we each have a part to play. There are some things that women excel in and some things that men do. We've got to stop looking at our own personal issues and think of what's best for the Church.'

Mrs Fox points out that the CWL is involved in all sorts of projects both within the Church and in the wider community. 'We work with everything under the sun. We have a great social concern. We work with refugees, in the prisons and the crèches. We are involved in working with the family, we look after our elderly people and many of our women work in the hospices. Our main purpose is, of course, education but we are involved in every aspect of community work.'

There's no doubt that Catholic women's groups like the CWL and the Union of Catholic Mothers undertake many vital activities. But no matter what they do or how hard they work, these groups do not represent 'real women' at all, claimed a 1983 information sheet published by the Newman Association Family Committee, which dismissed the major Catholic women's organizations in one paragraph.

The four-page 'Are Women Still Playing an Inferior Part in the Church?' conceded that the UCM and the CWL 'do a great deal of pastoral work on a neighbourly basis' but claimed that 'how far they are imbued with the spirit of Vatican II varies from branch to branch'. It summed up with the sweeping statement that 'in general these organizations are not much concerned with questions of sexual equality'.

'We're too busy to get involved in all of that,' says Pat Gough, the CWL's public relations officer. 'We're out there on the streets doing whatever it is we need to be doing instead of theorizing about it.'

Mrs Gough admits that sexual equality isn't high on her agenda but points out that the CWL's founder, Margaret Fletcher, became quite a feminist in her day by working for better educational opportunities for women. At a time when Catholic women could not go to university without permission from the local bishop, Margaret Fletcher set up houses where women could study without fear for their spiritual or moral welfare.

'It was around the time of the suffragette movement but Margaret Fletcher was very careful not to get involved in that,' Mrs Gough explains. 'She channelled all her energies into working for the Church and, with the backing of the Church, helped people who needed help.

'We've been involved in helping women with education ever since. Education is so much more available to women now and, thank God, there don't seem to be any barriers to that any more. But there are still areas where we can help, particularly for people who have not had the opportunity to go on to university and want to learn a bit more. This is why we have our connection with Plater College, Oxford, and grants available for people to go to summer school there.'

Mrs Gough says she doesn't understand those women who claim they are oppressed by a patriarchal Church and points out that the Church has been largely run and supported by women for years. 'There are more women going to church than men. If it wasn't for women teaching their kids, teaching them their prayers and taking them to church, where would we be? But I was at a conference once where there were women actually in tears because of the language of the Bible, because it wasn't PC enough for them. Personally I couldn't care less about the language of the Bible, it was written when it was written. I suppose it's how you feel about things and how far you want to push the whole feminism thing. The attitude of the priest can affect how you feel.

'I'm grateful to those [feminists] who were active in the sixties and seventies – I didn't always appreciate the way they went about it but what they did for women back then has given us what we've got today. In most places there is equality in the workplace and that is a legacy we've gained from the people of the sixties and seventies.

'I've never been stopped from doing anything I want to do. I think the only barrier now is the priesthood – and I don't want to be a priest.'

Maybe not, but there are plenty of women who do – admittedly some of them are the last people in the world you'd want as your priest, just as some of the most fervent anti-abortionists are the last people you'd trust to babysit the kiddies – and calls for 'sexual equality' soon became as common within the Church as they were in the secular world. Less than ten years after the Newman Association's report women were reportedly 'infiltrating' the upper echelons of the Bishops' Conference.

When, in 1992, the Church of England Synod finally voted to allow women to be ordained priests, the Catholic hierarchy of England & Wales expressed its 'profound regret' at the result. But two Catholic women's groups were delighted with the decision. The St Joan's International Alliance and the Catholic Women's Network (CWN) issued a joint statement welcoming the move.

Meanwhile the anti-feminists – most of them women – moved in for the kill. Before the Church of England could lay a beringed episcopal hand on its first female tonsure, Family Publications had produced *The Enemy Within*, which claimed that radical Catholic feminists were trying to win over the Catholic bishops to the idea of ordaining Catholic women too. The book claimed that the CWN had joined forces with the Catholic Lesbian Sisterhood at pagan ceremonies which included 'apple blessing' and 'green ribbon liturgy'.

It was impossible to read *The Enemy Within* without realizing that there are quite a few women in the Church who oppose women's ordination. The book pointed an accusing finger at one suspect in particular – Pat Jones, a theology graduate from Liverpool, then assistant general secretary to the Bishops' Conference. The fact that Ms Jones was a member of the CWN proved to Christine Kelly, the book's editor, that her appointment to the Bishops' Conference was simply an example of feminist infiltration.

'I've never been part of a conspiracy,' said Ms Jones at the time, 'and I think it would be very inappropriate. It's not pleasant to be written about in this way and it's such a ludicrous claim that I don't know if anyone could take it seriously. Who has time to sit around planning to infiltrate? There's too much to do. I object to the word "infiltrate" – I do everything openly. Anyone can ask me where I stand and I will tell them. My aim is more on the lines of women being more involved in the life of the Church. I am a member of CWN but I wouldn't say I agree with everyone in it.'

Admittedly some of the more militant women have done some totally daffy things in order to draw attention to their cause, such as disrupting the Maundy Thursday Chrism Mass at St David's Cathedral, Cardiff, in 1996 by standing on the cathedral steps singing hymns. Then there are the women who stood outside Westminster Cathedral on the First Sunday of Advent in 1995 to share their experiences of 'exclusion' from the Church. In a literally 'touching' gesture, they held their hands against the cathedral walls 'as a symbol of cleansing the Church from the sin of sexism'.

Such actions did little more than bring ridicule upon those men and women who were seriously debating the whole women's ordination issue. The activists provided plenty of ammunition for Catholic writer Joanna Bogle, who, under the pseudonym of Carmel Lenehan, sent a spoof article about Catholic women's activities in Australia to *Network*, the CWN's own magazine.

> We began with a foot massage and then, in a circle, we each in turn spoke, saying 'I matter. I affirm self. What I am, I have a right to be.' It was really moving. Over avocado and salads we shared music, and there was talk about the Church and the way it/he oppresses us and how we can change it.
>
> We heard from Sam who found that 'prayer means nothing – it just means hurt – if you can't be up there at the altar but only anonymous in the pew' and who is quietly, serenely, staying away from Church until this comes about, praying instead in the garden – or in a warm bath.

Joanna Bogle insists this was not just a joke and that there was a serious side to the piece. 'I simply read their other material and wrote my own. I deliberately made them over-indulgent and wallowing in ego massaging – everything that the Christian should not be. They didn't for one moment see that everything I was saying was totally contrary to the spirit of Christ and they published it. They fell for it hook, line and sinker. I can laugh at this and I did do it for fun. But I had a serious reason and I would not have done it except for there being a serious reason – it was not a prank and it was meant as a reproach to them.

'In my opinion it explained and summarized that they are a long, long way from the Catholic Church. The Catholic road is a good one to trudge but it does involve picking up your cross and trudging alongside Christ and it doesn't involve ego massaging.'

In March 1993, exactly a year before the Bristol ordinations, a group of Catholics held a silent 'Vigil of Mourning for Women's Lost Gifts' on the piazza of Westminster Cathedral. Walking in a circle 'as a symbol of equality between men and women' and wearing purple 'as a sign of permanent Lent for women's lost gifts and abilities within the Church', this group had very different aims from CWN's call for more involvement in the life of the Church. This was the official launch of Catholic Women's Ordination and their demand was clear – that women should be ordained to priesthood in the Roman Catholic Church.

The Bishops' Conference responded with a simple statement: 'Women's gifts are used in the Church in many different ways, in particular as teachers, catechists and eucharistic ministers. The Catholic Church does not consider itself authorized to admit women for ordination.' The following year, as those 32 women kneeled in Bristol Cathedral before Bishop Barry Rogerson to be 'priested', Pope John Paul, in an apostolic letter, confirmed that 'the Church has no authority whatsoever to confer priestly ordination on women'.

Despite Pope John Paul's pronouncement that the subject was closed, the campaign for women's ordination continued. In 1999 more than 22,000 Irish people signed a petition calling on the Church to admit women to holy orders and in Germany and Austria the We Are Church group was pushing hard for women's ordination. Europe's bishops, attending a synod in Rome in October, insisted that women 'must never be discriminated against again' and called for 'significant openings' to be made for women in the Church.

'Throughout Church history women have always been in the front line, in terms of teaching, solidarity, the family, or for having founded some of its great movements,' said Monsignor Aldo Giordano, secretary-general of the Council of European Bishops' Conferences. 'Yet we have not adequately recognized this. We are proposing that women's access to public functions in the Church be favoured in every way. We want a number of openings, ranging from participation in pastoral care in the parishes to responsibility in significant offices of the Roman Curia.'

With so many calls from groups that could be labelled 'left' or 'right', the average bishop could be forgiven for placing his head in his hands and begging for a bit of peace and quiet. While the more mainstream groups like the UCM and the CWL simply get on with the work, there's no doubt that it is the smaller fringe groups who are making all the noise.

All shades of opinion are represented on the National Board of Catholic Women (NBCW), a consultative body set up by the bishops of England & Wales just after the Second World War. The NBCW now consists of representatives of 35 Catholic organizations and, more recently, most of the bishops have appointed women from their own dioceses as their official links. The theory is that the Board should represent the most widely held views of Catholic women in dialogue with the bishops.

'The bishops are our pastoral leaders,' says NBCW development officer Angela Perkins. 'They are the guardians of orthodoxy in the Church and if women want to say anything about their role within the life and mission of the Church community, it must be in dialogue with the bishop.

'Our bishops are incredibly open and approachable. They have a willingness to listen and there's the distinct feeling that we are walking "arm in arm" with them – that's a phrase Cardinal Hume used in his address to the NBCW in December 1998.

'Of course there are women who think we are walking too fast and there are those who think we are not walking fast enough. The majority of organizations and dioceses in membership with the NBCW understand both extremes but we cannot allow the work of the board to be hijacked by minority views. Listening, understanding, dialogue is essential not only between women and men but between women themselves. That's the harmonizing role of the NBCW – however imperfectly some may feel it operates, at least it tries to provide that service to the Church.'

There's no doubt that the NBCW's service is appreciated. When the bishops of England & Wales went on their five-yearly visit to Rome in 1992, Pope John Paul commended the Board's work specifically. In 1996 the Pope said he 'sought to advance a dialogue, especially with women themselves, on what it means to be a woman in our time'. And Archbishop Pablo Puente, the Pope's representative in Britain, has said that women can participate 'in the great dialogue which is indispensable within the Church of the future century'.

But it all sounds rather patronizing, as though women are a case for special treatment. Why 'dialogue' with women in particular? Angela Perkins believes that now, more than ever, women have a real role to play in passing on belief to future generations: 'For 2000 years we have had a patriarchal world, a men-led world. That is changing. These men, with their important roles in the hierarchy of the Church, have recognized the need to understand the modern woman, the way she expects a relationship of equality with men and a developing role within the Church of the 21st century. They know women are silently slipping out of the Church and they know that when a woman leaves, the rest of the family usually leaves with her.

'Women still have that pivotal role in the practice of the faith. And that is why dialogue with women is so important.'

Shortly before his death, Cardinal Hume said that 'the decision makers are men, bishops and priests' and that 'many of the decisions they make directly affect women'.

'Women should be closely involved at different levels in the Church with decision making. How this could be brought about successfully I do not know, but in this area there is work to be done by us all. Dialogue is needed.'

All very well, says Josephine Robinson. But what are they talking about and what decisions are there to be made? 'Obviously people talking together is a good thing,' she says. 'But the difficulty for any women's organizations in dialogue with bishops is that it's a bit like trade union negotiation. The dialogue tends to assume a kind of quid pro quo. It's always about what concessions we can get out of the people we are in dialogue with and that isn't quite the kind of attitude that people should have in the Church.

'It's rather like the school council where the girls ask to wear their skirts two and a half inches above the knee and the next time they have a school council meeting they ask for five and a half inches. They keep pushing for more.

'The trouble with dialoguing with women is that it tends to have a rather political agenda. They always say they want to be part of the decision-making process in the Church. What decisions are they thinking of? So many of these things often have a subtext. Very often this is code for the ordination of women, liberalizing of things like divorce laws and reception of holy Communion by people in invalid unions.

'Now what is so important is the family matters, the pro-life matters, the things which are actually of specific interest to women. Women have a different way of looking at things because they bear the children and they have an essential responsibility in the first education of children. These are tremendously important issues.'

In 1995 Pope John Paul issued an open letter apologizing for any wrongs committed by the Catholic Church against women throughout history. He said humanity owed an unpayable debt to the 'great, immense feminine tradition' and mourned the fact that women were 'frequently at a disadvantage from the start, excluded from equal opportunities, underestimated, ignored and not given credit for their intellectual contributions'. He praised feminism and 'the great process of women's liberation', insisting that women were entitled to 'the recognition of everything that is part of the rights and duties of citizens in a democratic state'. But again, he stressed, only men could possibly fill the role of priest.

For one priest this was all too much. A few months later Father John Wijngaards resigned from the ministerial priesthood. A priest for 40 years, Wijngaards said he had become uncomfortable with the Church's teaching on artificial contraception, obligatory celibacy and homosexual partnerships.

'I'm not a rebel by nature,' says Wijngaards. 'But the question of women was the breaking point for me because I have been personally involved in theological research and pastoral ministry concerning this issue for the past 20 years.'

Wijngaards claims the argument that the priesthood should be male because the apostles were male doesn't hold water and points out there were no black apostles either. He refers to Greek and Syriac manuscripts from the fourth to the eighth centuries that contain ordination ceremonies for both male and female deacons. 'From the outset we should realize what is at stake. If, as records show, women were admitted to the full diaconate, which is now only imparted to men, then they did receive the sacrament of holy orders.

'The Church has made awful and costly mistakes in the past. The Congregation for Doctrine, for instance, declared in 1866 that slavery was not contrary to natural law and that slaves could legitimately be held, bought and sold. This doctrine of Pius IX was revoked by Leo XIII and utterly condemned by Vatican II.'

The feminist writer and lay theologian Sara Maitland left the Church of England around the time it began ordaining women. The wife of an Anglican priest – who followed her into the Catholic Church – she had no problem with the General Synod agreeing to the ordination of women but couldn't understand why they separated this from raising women to the episcopate.

'It seemed to me that was the first time anything explicitly sexist had been written into the constitution, as well as it being appallingly bad theology to separate bishops from priests,' she says. 'What they were saying is "priesthood's not as important as we thought it was", rather than "women are not as thick as we thought they were". I found that completely bizarre. It made me dislike the whole Church of England at an intense level.'

However, Sara does not accept the theory that the Catholic Church cannot change its teaching on the ordination of women. 'It changed the teaching about Gentiles and found it difficult to do. That's what the whole of the Acts of the Apostles is about in one sense, it's Peter and Paul arguing it out. And Paul wins. If Peter had won, the present Pope couldn't have been ordained because he is Polish, and there couldn't have been a church in Europe. If the Gospel or baptism had not been open to Gentiles, then there is no way the Church could have survived.

'I absolutely do not understand the Pope's declarations on women – the apology was good but what followed from that, about the special ministry of women, was completely peculiar. It seemed to me not to hold together at a logical level. It made the vocation of Christian women absolutely identical to the biological nature of women and he has always argued that we were not biologically restricted. I don't understand what he was saying.'

It is impossible to estimate how many Catholics are in favour of women's ordination or, at least, not against. There are probably many Catholics in the pew who, at least privately, dissent on issues such as contraception and gay relationships. It is only those who dare to stick their heads above the parapet who get shot at. One such person was Sister Lavinia Byrne, of the Institute of the Blessed Virgin Mary, whose 1994 book *Women at the Altar* came out in favour of the ordination of women and the relaxing of the rules governing artificial family planning. The book didn't exactly go down well in Vatican circles, the Congregation for the Doctrine of Faith demanding that she sign a document declaring her support of Church teaching on these issues. She refused and asked, 'after 18 months of pressure from the Vatican', to be dispensed from her vows and to leave the community.

She said at the time, 'I am profoundly sorry this is why I have to leave. I remain a loyal and committed member of the Roman Catholic Church and a supporter of my religious community. My quarrel is not with the Catholic Church in this country but with Rome. They are using techniques that seem to belong to another age. They are behaving like the Inquisition. I feel bullied. I am deeply saddened to have to leave a religious congregation which has a splendid record of championing the place of women in the Church and do so with great regret.

'Women do some of the most bold and adventurous work in the Church the world over, working with the poor, needy and disadvantaged as well as in universities, hospitals and schools. It is too easy to make them a sitting target by questioning their integrity and undermining their commitment to the Gospel.'

Dr Byrne claimed the Vatican's demands 'trivialized the faith' and said she intended to continue to lecture and write 'without constantly feeling that my integrity is being called into question'.

Pope John Paul has more than once reiterated the teaching that women cannot become priests because, quite simply, they cannot stand in the place of Christ, who was a man. It's an argument that faced little opposition in past centuries when men and women really did have different experiences and opportunities. But for many younger Catholics – even those who accept the teaching – it's hard to take on board that a man and woman can be that different. Whatever one's opinions on homosexuality, birth control, capital punishment and warfare, the Church's teaching on these subjects can be rationalized. But the belief that the two sexes are so different that only one of them can be ordained is a far deeper mystery to fathom than matters of faith like the Trinity or transubstantiation. The counter-argument is that, biblically speaking, God created both man and woman in his own image and likeness – but it's not difficult to find an out-of-context quote in the Bible to back up any belief or practice.

The other argument against the ordination of women is that Jesus Christ didn't choose any female apostles and the Church has maintained the tradition that, with one or two glitches, has served it adequately for the last 2,000 years.

Joanna Bogle fully accepts that women cannot be priests – she stresses it's a question of *cannot* rather than *may* not – but believes the debate will lead to a much richer understanding of 'why'. She cites the beliefs in the Trinity and the Eucharist that have been held from the very beginning of the Church but were only confirmed in the fourth and fifteenth centuries when opposed by heretics.

'We've known from the beginning that women could not be ordained,' she says, 'but it's only now we have a serious suggestion that women could be ordained, and the Church has to confront the heresy, that she will be forced to explore her doctrine more richly. I think a lot of very interesting and rather beautiful things will emerge – a theology of gender if you like.

'The debate on "why" has to assume that there *is* a teaching and that this teaching is worth exploring, not that there isn't a teaching or that the teaching will change. The tradition of asking "why" is very rich and very, very Catholic. And I think we're going to be richer for the debate about women priests.'

Sara Maitland says that she is unable to understand the arguments against the ordination of women. 'I can't see how you can argue it biblically. I don't see how you can argue it from St Paul because of the very clear definition that we are all one in baptism and therefore neither male nor female, Greek nor Jew.

'If you make men and women any more different than good sense allows, you get into problems of salvation. If we are saved by our assumption into Christ's crucifixion and resurrection, then if men and women are so different that they cannot share in the nature of the Church, I do not see how you get women saved at all. Saying it is absolutely impossible for women to be ordained raises many questions about whether they can be saved, even whether they can be baptized.'

The ACW's publicity material explains that the organization was founded because: 'Now more than ever before, Catholic women are facing very difficult questions. Their expectations of what life should offer have been raised to an impossibly high level. They are encouraged to work outside their homes and to challenge their role in the life of the Church'. So it comes as no surprise that chairman Josephine Robinson should consider the idea of ordaining women quite simply 'a no-no'.

'It doesn't mean women are inferior,' she explains. 'Men and women are equal before God but they have different functions. We think of motherhood with women, and the fact that men can bring Christ to the altar is a masculine thing. To have a woman doing it is quite literally a travesty, she is wearing the wrong clothes.'

The 1994 Catechism states: 'The Lord Jesus chose men to form the college of the 12 apostles and the apostles did the same when they chose collaborators to succeed them in their ministry. The Church recognizes herself to be bound by this choice made by the Lord himself and for this reason the ordination of women is not possible.' The present Pope has made it clear that the matter is simply not up for discussion – but it seems unlikely that a Church which changed its mind on slavery and capital punishment will, for much longer, be able to perpetuate the myth that men and women are fundamentally different.

✝

6. Crying Out to Heaven

On the Feast of Corpus Christi 1997, a 26-year-old man wearing a rainbow sash approached the altar rail at Westminster Cathedral to receive Communion. Cardinal Hume put down his ciborium, spoke to the man and walked away from him. The man returned to his bench.

That man was Nicholas Holloway, a homosexual who had forewarned the Cardinal of what he was planning to do. The Cardinal had responded that Westminster Cathedral was not the place to stage a protest.

The Church's rules on who can and can't receive Communion may appear pretty strict. But few people are ever refused publicly unless they cause 'scandal', as the rules quaintly describe it. In the 1960s two doctors who had founded family planning clinics were turned away from the communion rail, not so much because of their belief in artificial contraception but because they arrived at their respective churches with news crews and thereby risked causing a 'scandal'.

Similarly, Mr Holloway's intention was to make a public statement. He had been writing to Hume for months asking the Cardinal to state his position on whether 'practising homosexuals' could receive the Eucharist. The responses were non-committal. Cardinal Hume first advised Mr Holloway to consult his parish priest and then offered him an appointment to discuss the matter privately.

In May 1997 Mr Holloway published an 'open letter' to the Cardinal, stating that he would appear at Mass at Westminster Cathedral on the Feast of Corpus Christi wearing a rainbow sash, and would approach the Cardinal to receive Communion with outstretched arms, so being identifiable to Hume and others in attendance. The Cardinal was unhappy that Mr Holloway had gone public on the issue and responded in writing that, while he was still open to a meeting, he objected to 'the use of a sacred place or sacred moment to stage a demonstration by an individual or a group'.

'No one has the right to demand that the Church should publicly endorse their private decisions in conscience,' the Cardinal continued. 'That is what you have asked me to do. You cannot expect me to speak and act in contradiction to the Church's teaching on homosexual acts.'

Mr Holloway appeared as promised, and when he arrived at the front of the queue, the Cardinal told Mr Holloway that he had received his letter and would still be willing to meet with him to discuss the matter. The two men then walked in opposite directions.

Mr Holloway insists that he didn't expect or want the Church to change the rules. He simply wanted to make the point that the Church's attitude is like a family not accepting a favourite son's partner for the family meal. 'Initially the whole family spent years in gentle reflection and listening, sharing their points of view, respecting and honouring each other's experience and values,' he says. 'However, as time passed by it became clearer and clearer that here was a fundamentally contradictory set of values between the son and the father. The discussions and conversations began to wear away the relationships in the family. Meetings would end in anger, fury and sadness. People withdrew into their own positions. The situation became hopeless.

'Finally one Sunday the son, exhausted and frustrated by the years of exclusion, brought his lover into the house anyway and sat down at the family dinner table seeking to share in the meal. The father refused to serve them.'

Mr Holloway is convinced, however, that 'slowly and gently' the 'family' will come out and invite the son and his lover to join them again.

A few days after the Corpus Christi Mass, Cardinal Hume invited Nicholas Holloway to meet him privately. 'That afternoon the Cardinal listened deeply as he asked me about my experience of life and I shared with him some of the joy and pain of being alive,' Mr Holloway recalls. 'I don't think any other person has made such a deep impression on me. Cardinal Hume had a consistent message in his response to the rainbow sash. He said the action was "inappropriate" because the place and time of holy Communion is "sacred". It took me some years of listening to finally accept that for the Cardinal this remained a deeply held value.'

We can't know what Cardinal Hume's reaction would have been if approached by a man he knew to be gay but who was not making a public statement. Presumably he would have given Communion to such a person as, under canon law, no minister can refuse someone who approaches in good faith. The minister – lay or ordained – cannot assume someone is unworthy; to use the terminology of the Bishops' Conference document *Pastoral Care of Homosexual People*, 'culpability cannot be immediately assumed'. At the same time, if someone is known to be in a state of public conflict with the Church then giving them Communion may cause the aforementioned 'scandal'. There was some discussion on this when a priest refused to take Communion to General Pinochet under house arrest in Surrey and again when it was revealed that Yorkshire Ripper Peter Sutcliffe had been receiving Communion in prison.

Cardinal Hume's reaction was certainly more tolerant than that of Scotland's Cardinal Thomas Winning, who, speaking during the Section 28 debate in January 2000, said of homosexuality: 'I hesitate to use the word perversion but let's face up to the truth. I have no objection to anybody – I'm supposed to love my neighbour and I try to do that as much as I can. But I will not stand for this kind of behaviour which is now being regarded as wholesome and healthy.'

Not surprisingly, Cardinal Winning's words were attacked by many people who considered them offensive to a large section of the community. Even the Prime Minister, Tony Blair, made an oblique reference to his comments in the House of Commons.

And a letter to the *Independent* newspaper signed by 49 Catholics from all walks of life described the Cardinal's comments as 'stumbling blocks', 'in danger of legitimizing homophobic violence' and 'falling little short of incitement to hatred'. It went on to call upon 'our fellow Catholics in both Houses of Parliament to support the repeal of Section 28 and other discriminatory laws. Society and Church must stem the current tide of fearful hatred, move beyond mere tolerance and celebrate that diversity which is the mark of healthy and mature communities.'

Archbishop Cormac's words on taking up office were much more measured. He simply called on the Government to 'ensure that they kept the promise to teach the primacy of family life'.

Cardinal Hume, in his 'observations' on the Church's teaching on gay people, stressed that 'the Church recognizes the dignity of all people' regardless of their sexual orientation:

> In upholding the dignity of people who are homosexual the Church is not being inconsistent or false to its teaching. The Church has always taught that the genital expression of love is intended by God's Plan of creation to find its place exclusively within marriage between a man and a woman. The Church therefore cannot in any way equate a homosexual partnership with a heterosexual partnership, with a heterosexual marriage.
>
> Homosexual genital acts are objectively wrong, although the Church warns against generalization in attributing culpability in individual cases. The particular inclination of the homosexual person is not a sin. An inclination is not a sin. Being a homosexual person is neither morally good nor morally bad – it is homosexual genital acts that are morally wrong.

This is all hair-splitting stuff for Aidan and Nakul, a couple in their thirties who have been together for seven years. Aidan, a cradle Catholic, is a former member of a religious order. Nakul is a practising Hindu who is supportive and understanding of

Aidan's faith. Neither of them is looking for a gay marriage but they would like to see their relationship acknowledged in law for reasons of tax and inheritance.

'When I was studying canon law we were doing the section on marriage,' Aidan recalls. 'At the time a paralysed man in a wheelchair had just been married. We were told that marriage is one of the seven sacraments but unless it is consummated, unless there is actual penetration, it is not a sacramental marriage. I remember being appalled at that, that it took the physical act of sex to make something sacramental. We're always being told about the importance of family and relationships, respect and mutual understanding, and yet when it came down to it this man's marriage was not recognized by the Church because they couldn't have sex. I remember sitting there in the classroom – it was one of the pivotal points that made me realize I was going to have difficulties with the Church if I carried on training.'

Aidan believes certain sexual relationships were outlawed in the early years of Christianity when the newly emerging Church was trying to distance itself from pagan rites that included male and female prostitution.

'The early Christians really believed that Christ was going to come back very soon,' he explains. 'Obviously that didn't occur. But the idea of keeping themselves pure for the kingdom of heaven gradually became the accepted norm. Because Christ didn't come back as was expected they had to procreate, so they had to sanction some sorts of sexual activity while vilifying others.'

It's the great demon of sex that makes the relationship between Aidan and Nakul unacceptable to the Church. But Aidan is keen to stress that, as with any other couple, sex is far from being the focal point of their lives. They are still together after seven years because of mutual trust, support and understanding.

'We're best of friends,' he says. 'We love each other. We've recently been apart for a week because of work. That's the longest time we've been apart in the seven years and we really did miss each other a great deal. I can't see myself spending time with anybody else. The sex is pretty good but after seven years it's only part of the relationship. We do everything together. We don't do anything without asking each other. Even nights out tend to be done together.'

Take the Church out of the equation and for Aidan there is no problem. 'I came through all the Catholic guilt years ago. After three years of developing the spiritual life in a monastic situation, and coming across many good men and women, it made me realize that I think God isn't hung up on picky details on who you love and who you share your bed with.'

Maybe not, but the Church is. And gay Catholics working in Church jobs really do have to keep their heads down.

'Stephen', 34, is one of three gay teachers in a Catholic sixth-form college. They have all signed contracts that say they will do nothing to bring the Catholic Church into disrepute. It is this clause that the governors could use if his sexuality was considered a problem.

'It's a weak argument,' says Stephen, who is genuinely scared for the future of his job if he reveals his real name. 'If it ever came out I would argue my point and embarrass the principal and the governors because then I would be more vocal about my sexuality. I think they can argue that line but it's not just a gay issue. Not only are there gay staff, there are heterosexual members of staff who are living with someone.'

So Stephen has to be careful about who does and doesn't know he is gay, a situation that would not arise in many non-Catholic state schools where gay teachers can bring their partners to social gatherings the same as anyone else. 'I am not out but I haven't hidden anything,' he says. 'I choose who to tell and our chaplain is fine about the issue. But if I have a partner I can't bring him to a staff party. The whole Catholic ethos seems to focus around families, children and opposite-sex partners. Under any Christian organization you can almost justify homophobia by your faith alone or by what the Church teaches.'

Stephen points out that, while the Church continues to stress the ethics of homosexuality, there is a large number of gay RE teachers, gay nurses and gay priests. 'It may be a stereotype,' he says, 'but perhaps it's because we are more able to express our feelings and our emotions, and that goes with our faith and our spirituality as well. I'm part of the Church and they've got me. I have as much right to be part of it as anyone else.'

To the uninitiated, the concept of gay priests can come as a bit of a shock. We only hear about them if they break the rules, like the priest who had a heart attack in the presumed anonymity of a gay sauna and was given the last rites by a fellow cleric who just happened to be on site. But the great majority of gay priests are as celibate as their heterosexual brothers, and they still have to keep their sexuality a secret because of public preconceptions about how gay people live.

'Father Benjamin' is quite open about his sexuality with most of his priest friends and his superior knows he is gay. But he is more cagey with parishioners, particularly the older generation who would find it much more difficult to take on board.

'Recently two of my friends, daily Mass-goers, wonderfully kind open people, were telling me how much they appreciated Cardinal Winning's stand for the truth, and how priests should speak out more against homosexuality,' he says. 'I believe a lot of ordinary Catholics think that way, so one is less than inclined to come out publicly if that would invite rejection. Also I would be somewhat wary of causing scandal – if you make it more difficult for your flock to approach you, then you are not really doing your job.

'This can cut both ways. It's extraordinary how people under-stand "gay" – often people hear something like "active" or "promiscuous". Until a few years ago I carefully made the dis-tinction myself, saying I was homosexual but not gay, because the latter implied a lifestyle I do not practise and a set of attitudes I did not share. But I've found the distinction blurred somewhat in the intervening years. When I say I'm gay I'm talking about my sexual orientation – full stop – not the way I live.'

Father Benjamin points out that, until recently, priests were very reluctant to discuss, or even consider, their own sexual feel-ings and that most Catholics supposed their priests were not sexual beings. 'If all the gay priests really did stand up and be counted you would be dealing with 30 or 40 per cent,' he says, 'and that, for some people, would not look good. Many priests simply don't face their sexuality. They never really have to ask the questions, and when they hear about other gay priests it brings them that little bit closer to having to face the truth about themselves. But I think in this day and age it is increasingly difficult not to be sexually aware.'

Father Benjamin says there is also 'a degree of denial' that 'masquerades' as orthodoxy. 'Walk around Rome and you will see young men dressed up like the Curé of Ars, looking very much the part of the ideal priest or seminarian,' he says. 'You can tell by the way some of them walk and talk that they are as camp as a row of pink tents. This traditional image of priesthood is a very powerful, clear persona and can give one a very strong sense of identity. Sometimes that is exactly what a young gay man wants. Because his own real identity is so confused or even – in his own eyes – sinful, he is very happy to find another identity that he thinks everybody loves.

'This type of priest is very likely to lead a double life. In public very orthodox, strait-laced, often even rigid, unpleasantly traditional and likely to preach against the evils of homosexuality. In private sexually active. As someone once said to me, "lace by day, leather by night".

'Some people are delighted to see groups of young priests and seminarians walking round like this and think it is some sort of return to traditional Catholicism. It is in fact nothing of the sort. It has the trappings of traditional Catholicism but these are people who live the moral code in their public lives – privately they are right little ravers.'

Father Benjamin stresses that not all these young priests are necessarily living double lives. He knows many gay priests who are well adjusted and suited to their chosen lifestyle and are 'living out their priesthood as best they can'. He is critical of 'our prurient society' where 'everybody wants to know everything about each other's sexuality'. He adds: 'While some of the reticence, even silence, in the Church on these issues is born of denial and a refusal to face the facts, some of it is the product of a wisdom much older than that of our age, that says basically that a person's sexuality is nobody's business but his own.'

For nearly 30 years Quest, a lay organization of gay Catholics, has enjoyed a reasonable relationship with the bishops of England & Wales. In most dioceses they meet on a monthly basis for Mass and social activities, and local groups are listed in diocesan yearbooks. Several bishops have attended Quest's annual summer conference and some have even spoken to this national gathering.

Cardinal Hume had met with members of Quest's national council and had approved their aims to 'sustain and increase Christian faith among homosexual men and women' as listed in the *National Catholic Directory*, an official guide to the Church in England & Wales published with the authority of the Bishops' Conference. All was well until, in the mid-1990s, someone drew the Cardinal's attention to a clause in Quest's official constitution that spoke of 'the full expression of their homosexual nature in loving Christian relationships'. Whoops! Sex had reared its beautiful head again.

The Cardinal immediately demanded to know whether Quest supported Church teaching that genital acts outside marriage are wrong. Did it encourage its members to live accordingly? And, if so, what did it mean by including a clause in its constitution that appeared to back relationships akin to heterosexual marriage? Quest, which counts a number of priests and theologians among its membership, met the Cardinal head on, arguing in skilful theological language while at the same time avoiding the direct question with all the craft of the most evasive politician.

For the next four years the debate raged. The Cardinal met with members of Quest. Members of Quest met with each other. Letters flew around the country. Quest debated the clause in question and decided no – enough was enough and they would not alter this part of their constitution.

By the end of 1998, an exasperated Cardinal acted, banning Quest from the 1999 *National Catholic Directory*. 'Quest's suspension from the Catholic Directory does not mean the exclusion of its members from the Catholic Church,' he stated. 'I would want to emphasize very strongly that the Church's pastoral concern for all the members of Quest remains undiminished. The

Church does not reject homosexual people even if they are practising, though it cannot condone what they are doing. Furthermore, bishops, priests and others, whilst upholding the teaching of the Church, must nonetheless be understanding, sympathetic and helpful. It has not always been so in the past.'

Cardinal Hume's supporters claim he acted under pressure from Rome, following the complaints of more conservative groups who were themselves under threat of exclusion.

'Some of the bishops feel they have been misled,' explains Martin Pendergast, co-ordinator of Celebrating Catholic Diversity. 'The bishops can't be seen to continue overt and active support for Quest as Quest's members are on record as having a majority who reject Church teaching on the subject. They can't support the Roman Catholic Caucus in the Lesbian and Gay Christian Movement which openly dissents from Catholic teaching in its statement of conviction. And the bishops have nothing of their own to offer.'

In short, it's OK to be gay and Catholic – as long as you don't make a song and dance about it. Even St Thomas Aquinas acknowledged that homosexuality was a perfectly natural phenomenon, provided you lived within certain parameters. Yes, there have been one or two ecclesiastically approved hangings and burnings. But for the last few hundred years – with one or two hiccups – the Catholic Church, while the secular world was executing, imprisoning and lambasting homosexuals, has spoken up for the equality of all.

Many gay people ignore the rules and carry on with their relationships while remaining practising members of the Church. Some bend the rules a little. Others deprive themselves of the sacraments so they can continue to remain in the Church and in their relationships. And there are those who simply turn their backs on their religious background.

'I've not abandoned God,' explains Michael Holland, a 36-year-old graphic designer, 'but I've more or less abandoned the Church. My priest told me I had to choose sex or holy Communion. It was as though sex was something on its own, something that could be taken out of our relationship. Something evil that was eating away at me.

'He even told me that it was more or less OK to sleep around. That, he said, was "hot-blooded" and not premeditated and therefore was a forgivable sin. But continuing in my relationship with Christopher meant that I had no intention of changing my ways and therefore I was "living in sin".

'I've always accepted that the Church has rules – it has to. But I find it difficult to believe that priest was willing to let me walk out of the Church forever, rather than admit that perhaps God is a little bit bigger than the rules and regulations.

'I've not lost my faith – not in God, anyway. But I can't say I believe in the Church much any more. If my priest had even told me I was falling short of the ideal I could have coped with that. But to tell me that making love with my partner, with whom I share everything, was "living in sin" and beyond God's forgiveness, made me question the whole shooting match.

'I still occasionally go to Mass and holy Communion – it's all too important to me to abandon it altogether. But I go to churches where I am not known, where nobody knows that I have a happy home life. In one church the priest must have recognized a kindred spirit and he chatted me up after Mass – now that really made me sick. That guy has taken a promise of celibacy. I haven't. And yet, officially, I can't receive the sacraments, while he was up there presiding over the whole thing. I cried when I got home.

'Christopher is an atheist. For years he has supported me, putting up with me going to all the Holy Week services when he'd rather we went away together for a few days' Easter holiday. He's always said that as it was something I believed in, then he would back me up – he even came to church with me a few times. But when all this happened he just said, "You've got to get out – it's not going to do you any good." He tried to understand but he can't. How *can* he? He wasn't brought up to it the way I was.'

Michael Carson, author of the classic gay Catholic novel *Sucking Sherbet Lemons*, agrees. 'One of the problems with the Church's totally negative attitudes to homosexuality is that they encourage promiscuity. It is easier for a Catholic homosexual to fall occasionally into the bushes than to live openly with one partner.'

Carson remembers having the rules rammed home, learning them by rote from *The Penny Catechism*. Try as he might he can't get away from them. It's like an addiction, he says, although these days he's rather choosy about which bits he uses to feed his habit. 'Being a Catholic is as much part of culture as it is a religion,' he says. 'It's part of one's cultural inheritance and identity and one does not give up on it – that would mean giving up on many precious hand-me-downs.

'I was away from church-going for 20 years or more. I would not say that I am fully back and do not expect to be. I guess I will not allow institutional Catholicism to take over. I am a picky eater where Catholicism is concerned. If you've been fed so much junk food by them, it makes you "à la carte". I suppose I have discovered the Reformation three or four hundred years after a lot of my compatriots.'

For Mr Carson, the 'junk food' was fried, boiled, stewed and dished out by the Christian Brothers at an all-boys grammar school. These days the few brothers left have stood down in favour of lay staff and concentrate their efforts on their original calling of working with poor youngsters at home and abroad. But in Carson's days in 4B they were serving up *The Penny Catechism* with a starter of purity and a main course about sodomy being one of the four sins 'crying to heaven for vengeance'.

'It made you feel maggoty,' he recalls. 'It made you despise yourself and feel dirty. It also went a long way to stunting my sexual life – and, in common with many a Catholic, gay and straight, male and female, sex is something I can never be comfortable with.' Carson's memories are depressingly like those of his namesake Michael, the gay Catholic character in Matt Crowley's 1969 stage play *The Boys in the Band*: 'You show me a happy homosexual and I'll show you a gay corpse.'

The wind of Vatican II blew out the flames below the great stewpots of the Christian Brothers and many other teaching orders. For many of Carson's contemporaries – particularly his gay contemporaries – this was a wind of change, a wind that carried choice and freedom on its breath. And they voted with their feet.

'It was very odd in those days,' he says. 'One side of people was shocked that such change could happen. The sins of one's childhood – eating meat on Fridays, missing Mass, attending Protestant churches – ceased to be sins. There was a hole in the dyke. Catholics of that era were not great critical thinkers. So much that should have been discussed with openness could not be because of the whiff of sin and judgement and horrors hereafter.

'But I do not think that the Catholic Church has yet made the required leap to understand homosexuality. It's a church that suits the legalistic types but needs to open itself up to loving responses that people within the institution already know.'

The whole question of homosexuality is a hot potato for Catholic churchmen in England and Wales. While lay groups like Pro Ecclesia et Pontifice and Family and Youth Concern hold their hands up in horror at any mention of the word 'gay', the bishops have constantly made it clear that while the gift of sex is not intended for homosexual activity, gay people – and even gay relationships – are not to be condemned. Of course, this has led to a few battles over the years.

When, in 1993, Edwina Currie proposed lowering the age of consent for gay men to 18, Daphne McLeod of Pro Ecclesia said the move was 'legalizing child abuse', while Dr Liz Stuart of the Catholic Caucus of the Lesbian and Gay Christians said it was 'a basic elimination of injustice'. Meanwhile Cardinal Hume simply asked Parliament to be 'cautious' in its deliberations, while reiterating his earlier condemnation of homophobia:

> The Church teaches that being a homosexual person is
> neither morally good nor morally bad. Whatever the age
> of consent, Catholic teaching remains that homosexual
> genital acts are morally wrong. But the Church con-
> demns the use of violence of speech or action against
> homosexual people. The Church teaches that we are all of

equal value in the sight of God by virtue of our common humanity.

The Church does not expect that acts that are morally wrong should, by that fact alone, be made criminal offences. In general, it is neither practical nor desirable that everything immoral be made illegal. Thus adultery is clearly immoral, but it would be difficult in our society to make it illegal.

He did, however, ask Parliament to 'seek to protect young people and promote moral values that society recognizes as wholesome'.

The House of Commons voted in favour of Edwina Currie's amendment, although there was opposition in the House of Lords when Catholic peers Lord Longford and the Duke of Norfolk joined forces to reverse the motion. And when, in June 1998, the debate returned to the House of Commons, this time with a view to bringing the age of consent between gay men in line with the legal age for heterosexuals and gay women, the *Catholic Herald* 'named and shamed' Catholic MPs who had backed the motion that 'marked a new low in this country's slide into moral degeneracy'. The paper's leader writer wrote:

> Our political representatives have chosen to side with a vociferous and unrepresentative minority. Their political correctness may be faultless. Their betrayal of the people's trust is not. For Roman Catholic MPs slavishly to follow the Labour line, regardless of the damage done to young people, is the more reprehensible. Only by action in the House of Lords can the new measures be challenged. Their Lordships need the courage which their Commons colleagues signally lacked.

Strong stuff from a Catholic paper. But not quite as vitriolic as the words from so-called family campaigner Valerie Riches of Family and Youth Concern, who told the *Catholic Herald* that 'homosexuality and paedophilia are closely linked'.

The Union of Catholic Mothers took a less condemnatory line in 1999 when the Government announced plans to give gay partnerships the same legal status as those of straight couples, including the right to inherit a dead partner's estate and to insure a partner's life. Janette Woodford, then national president of the UCM, agreed – while standing up for traditional Church teaching on marriage – that it might be necessary to give gay couples some sort of legal protection: 'We don't seek to condemn, but we do want to recognize and honour those who are willing to stand up and be publicly counted for their intention to create a permanent, stable marriage and family.

'We do not believe that same-sex partnerships show respect for the Maker's instructions and we therefore don't think they should expect the rights which are properly attributable to those who accept the responsibilities of the created sexuality – male and female, united in love and open to new life.' She added that it might be preferable to add a new law to the statute books rather than changing 'the existing law to be all-embracing when the situations are not'.

'The Church is called to be both mother and teacher,' explains Father Tony Churchill, a moral theologian in Arundel & Brighton diocese. 'As a teacher the Church has to set the ideals clearly and without compromise, but as a mother the Church has to apply those to the actual situation of people. Without in any way deviating from the teaching of the Church, you can be extremely practical, pastorally kind and gentle and helpful.'

This was Archbishop Cormac's attitude throughout his time in Arundel & Brighton. He is known to be far from homophobic and the only time he turned down a gay man seeking ordination was when he doubted the candidate's ability to cope with compulsory celibacy. There hasn't been a branch of Quest in Archbishop Cormac's old diocese for several years, but he cared enough about gay people to appoint Father Churchill as a liaison between Quest, the diocese and gay people in the area.

'Archbishop Cormac was always clear about the teaching of the Church and he never attempted in any way to challenge that,' says Father Churchill, 'but he was equally pastoral in practical situations. He was extremely compassionate and understanding in dealing with individuals.'

In London there are several branches of Quest serving gay Catholics in the north, south, east and west districts, drawn from the dioceses of Westminster, Southwark and Brentwood. The central London groups come together in a Westminster parish once a month for a meeting or discussion and there are also monthly house Masses. So there's every chance that what has been a low-key issue in Archbishop Cormac's old diocese, will be a much more public affair in his new one.

Father Churchill says the Archbishop is well able to stand by the Church's teachings while remaining pastoral and approachable to the people concerned. 'Cormac sees these various teachings as a prophetic call to live a holy life and in that sense the Church shouldn't compromise on its ideals,' says Father Churchill. 'But, having said that, you have to apply it with great pastoral sensitivity. Like Cardinal Hume, he was very much influenced by Pope Paul VI in that kind of approach. In *Humanae Vitae*, having set out the principles, Pope Paul says that people who come to the priest must find in him an echo of the love of the redeemer, the compassion of our Lord. And that is very much Cormac's approach, very pastoral and gentle.'

The Vatican has gone to great lengths to explain that gay sex acts are unacceptable as they are not open to the creation of new life. Cardinal Hume and the bishops of England & Wales, while stressing the dignity of gay people, further expounded the theory. The suggestion is that heterosexual sex is OK because it is open to conception. Of course this is far from the case. The only straight sex act that can lead to pregnancy is penetration; presumably, then, there is no moral difference between gay sex and the many straight sex acts that cannot lead to conception. So there is still some discrimination against gay Catholics – or perhaps Church leaders are rather naïve about what really goes on in the heterosexual bedrooms of Britain.

✢

7. Some Definite Service

During Archbishop Cormac's time as vocations director in Portsmouth, quite a number of young men in the diocese were offering themselves for the priesthood. This was in the mid-1960s when there were perhaps more clerical students than at any time before or since, reaching a peak in the number of priests in England & Wales in the early 1970s. Those who knew him at the time say that Archbishop Cormac's particular contribution was his own good example.

But times have changed and we no longer have as many priests or nuns as we had 30 years ago. There are plenty of explanations for this, the most common being that there are far fewer people in the pews and so, per head of Mass-going Catholics, we're not doing too badly. Other explanations include the rise of consumerism and the greater number of choices for young people – particularly young women – today. And there's even the daring suggestion that, just possibly, the Holy Spirit is wafting through the Church trying to stir up lay people to realize their own callings and take on more responsibility for the life of the Church. In the words of Cardinal John Henry Newman:

> God has created me to do him some definite service. He has commissioned some work to me which he has not committed to another. I have my mission. I have a part in

this great work, I am a link in the chain. I ask not to see, I ask not to know. I ask simply to be used.

It's a philosophy that Archbishop Cormac certainly accepts, having been involved in initiatives with lay ministry from his time as a young priest in Portsmouth to more recent schemes in Arundel & Brighton diocese. But the former Rector of the English College, Rome, stresses that as more lay people become responsible for aspects of Church life, 'there is an even greater need' for priests to lead them:

> Often we limit our thoughts about the word 'vocation' to the priesthood or the consecrated life. These are essential elements of the life of the Church but they are not the whole picture. By virtue of our baptism all of us are called to hear the voice of Christ, the Good Shepherd, leading us and guiding us.
>
> The ever growing number of lay people who are taking responsibility for the life of the Church means that there is an even greater need for the ministry of the priest. The priest is engaged with the people in the building of an authentic Christian community.
>
> Ordination makes the priest a pivotal person in the parish and the way he assumes his responsibility of spiritual leadership is crucial. Then there is a challenge to the priest to develop a collaborative style of ministry with his bishop, fellow priests, religious and lay people. This is not always easy but it is the key to fruitful priestly service in the Church.

But Archbishop Cormac adds that there is 'an urgent need' for the whole Catholic community to recapture a new sense of vocation:

> Quite simply, we are and should be a vocational community that listens attentively to the voice of our risen Lord and responds generously. Of course I want to see more priests and religious and there must be an urgent appeal

to God for this to happen. However, I do not think this call will be fully answered unless we also concentrate on the vocation of every Christian by virtue of their baptism.

His words will be welcomed by many people including the writer Sara Maitland, who says that, on being received into the Catholic Church, she was shocked by 'how extraordinarily priest-dominated the laity are'. She finds this a far bigger, and more divisive, split than the rules that bar women from ordained ministry. 'The gulf in the Catholic Church between priest and lay is more serious, and more weird and more distorting, than the gap between who can and can't be in the priestly caste,' she says. 'The power is not men over women, it's clergy over laity in the Church. If there's a shortage of priests it's because they're doing all sorts of things that they needn't be doing. I find it quite strange that you never hear lay people preaching.'

Father Patrick Browne, vocations promoter in Westminster Archdiocese, agrees that it is time for priests to look at their ministry and how they work with lay people. He is encouraged by the rising number of enquiries he receives – in 1999, Westminster doubled its first-year student intake – although he says it's only 'a slight increase so I wouldn't hype it up'. Even so, he stresses that this is 'the most exciting time to be around'.

'The model of priesthood and the way we exercise our ministry have to change,' he points out. 'We have to be much more in collaboration with the lay people, who own the Church as much as we do and have just as great responsibility for preaching the Gospel as we do. We all have to work much more together, rather than we leading and expecting them to follow.'

When Archbishop Cormac began his ecclesiastical studies nearly 50 years ago he would have been surrounded by young men of roughly the same age. Most would have been 18 and a large number would have come from junior seminaries. The older ones would have been to university or done military service and few would have been past 25. Anyone older would have been considered 'a late vocation'.

These days the profile of candidates is quite different and much more wide-ranging. The men who began their studies for Westminster archdiocese in autumn 1999 were aged between 23 and 46 and included three teachers, a barrister, a bar man, a social worker and a doctor. Most men beginning seminary training these days will have had established jobs and private lives, experiences that will surely enrich the Church. But Father Browne insists it is how these experiences are used that counts.

'People jump to the conclusion that it's better that these men are older nowadays,' he says. 'That's neither right nor wrong. But we are very careful in our selection process that the people we take are the sort of people who have integrated their experience, have reflected on it and are the richer for it, rather than someone who's just been hurt, become embittered and puts all his rubbish on other people.

'Many of these people will have been in relationships and some of them will have been in sexual relationships, so there's a sense that they've been there and done that. If we accept them, hopefully they can look back on those experiences positively. You don't want people who are disgruntled by the whole thing, who are just negative.'

Father Browne says he is looking for people who have used their experiences to help them to a deeper understanding of themselves, of God and of other people. But he doesn't rule out younger students. 'You can't be exclusive about it. The Gospel is an ideal and if that can't appeal to the idealism of young people as well, to such an extent that they want to give themselves to living the Gospel and preaching it to others, then there's something sadly wrong.'

Father Jim O'Keefe, president of Ushaw College, County Durham, is also rejoicing in a recent rise in numbers but, again, he teaches his students that there is a vital relationship between 'the lay faithful, the ministerial priest and the consecrated religious, and you can't take any one out of the context of the rest of them'.

In September 1999 Ushaw, in common with the other six seminaries serving England & Wales, had a bigger intake than any other year in the last decade. Not that the seminaries are bursting at the seams – Ushaw has a total of 39 students rattling around in a building that once housed 11 times that number – but with a third of those 1999 students being first-years the increase is notable.

'It's not massive in terms of numbers but it's a significant increase in terms of the small numbers that we have,' says Father O'Keefe. 'When I was a student here myself in the mid-sixties there were 450 of us. That included a junior seminary up to the age of 18 and there were about 200 in the senior seminary.'

The average age of seminarians at Ushaw these days is around 30 – when Father O'Keefe was ordained in 1972 the eldest in his year was 25 and many had come from junior seminaries. These days men of all ages come from all walks of life, bringing much useful experience into the college and, subsequently, into their priesthood.

'Having lived longer and having a broader life in a family or in the world generally can be a terrific asset,' says Father O'Keefe. 'Fundamentally it does depend on what kind of church community you come from, because it can take as much energy to help someone broaden their understanding of what the Church is about as it did to encourage 18-year-olds to grow up.

'A lot depends on the person's background, on someone's family relationships and personal relationships over the last few years, on how comfortable they are with community life, with the notion of celibacy, with the simpler lifestyle. Those become very important questions that weren't around in the sixties and seventies, when a significant number of guys who were ordained came from junior seminaries.

'It depends on what the local parish community is like, how broad a notion of Church they have. If it's quite a narrow environment, or quite a narrow Church background, then that comes with them, it doesn't matter how old they are.'

Candidates spend time with their diocesan vocations directors and with other hopefuls before they attend a weekend at a seminary. There they speak to a panel of priests and lay men and women who provide the diocesan bishop with an advisory report.

They are given a psychological assessment and a medical and then have a formal meeting with the bishop and his advisors, who decide the best kind of formation – if any – for that person.

Once they begin their studies, students undergo an annual assessment process. But Father O'Keefe stresses that it's not a question of simply following the rules and not doing anything wrong in order to move up into the next year. 'There need to be good and positive reasons for someone moving on to the next stage of formation rather than a lack of negative indicators,' he says. 'If somebody hasn't done anything wrong, that doesn't count. There's got to be growth and maturity. A bit more wisdom and a bit more commitment.

'It's important that they have a broad notion of Church. There needs to be a deepening and a broadening of faith, not just an enthusiasm about the Gospel. There needs to be wisdom and learning. There's no harm in having a bit of energy and imagination but it's important that the enthusiasm is harnessed to being well informed as much as being well intentioned.

'A well-intentioned, enthusiastic leader could cause total havoc unless he was well informed and able to work collaboratively. I think that would be an essential characteristic now, that priests are able to work collaboratively with lay men and women and not be lone figures.'

Given the changing profile and rising age of the would-be seminarian, it's unlikely that many 18-year-olds will be starting their studies at Ushaw – or anywhere else for that matter – next autumn. Most contemporary A-level students are considering professional careers or beginning university courses.

Back to those sixth-formers at St Mary's College, Wallasey, who generally agreed that priesthood and religious life involved 'too much commitment'. The school has nurtured quite a few aspirant priests and religious over the last 30 years. All of those interviewed in February 2000 had spent around 12 years in Catholic schools and more than half were studying A level theology. They were amazed to discover that in days gone by, lads much younger than themselves – including their own teacher –

had been packed off to junior seminary. Only one of the boys, Steve, had briefly considered priesthood as a viable option before deciding that 'this kind of life seems lonely'.

Another, Ian, blamed the Tory dream for the fall in vocations: 'Today's society is driven by the selfish desire that capitalism offers,' he said. 'We are force fed a diet of commercials and are offered designer brands and materialistic gain. There is no emphasis on social behaviour or being a good member of society. People are taught to desire big houses and fast cars, not self-satisfaction and a sense of well-being. This is why the number of priests has reduced, as it seems a less attractive deal than the materialistic world we live in.'

Ian's words are not very far removed from those of Father Timothy Radcliffe, Master General of the Dominicans, who has said that 'the basic institutions of civil society that sustained the professions and vocations have lost much of their authority and independence. Like everything else, they must submit to market forces. In England, even a football team exists now less to play football than to make profit.' Or, as the philosopher Nicholas Boyle has written: 'There are no vocations for anyone any more. Society is not composed of people who have lives which they commit in this or that particular way, but of functions to be performed only as long as there is a desire to be satisfied.'

As Archbishop Cormac has said:

> There is great goodwill and goodness in our society but it is true to say that Christian practice and the Christian message have been diminished in England & Wales over recent years. While there is nothing that can take its place an attempt has been made by, among others, the culture of consumerism. This is a seduction that assumes that everything can be bought and sold and that even human beings are assessed by what they have rather than who they are.
>
> The Church believes that Christian faith is the potent force that allows us to be freed from a view of the world that ultimately can enslave us. The people of our country

have to learn again what it is to wonder at the gifts of God. We are to worship him alone and to teach each other, brothers and sisters, in a particular way to be on the side of those who are in most need.

Sister Margaret O'Ryan is one of those religious whose vocation has changed to meet the contemporary needs of society. She has seen a definite change of culture since the day, 50 years ago, when she entered the convent of the Holy Family and became one sister among many in a busy teaching order. Now living in a tower block on the outskirts of Liverpool, she believes that, with so much on offer, youngsters today find it difficult to make the necessary commitment to a particular way of life: 'You can't have your cake and eat it,' she says. 'You can't choose to do one thing and hanker after another, you have to make a commitment. And I find a lot of people today can't make that commitment.'

When she first decided on a religious life she was supported by the prevailing culture. 'We had a different attitude,' she says. 'We wanted something, we had a goal and we were aiming at it. In those days, because of the culture of the time, you didn't mind what you had to go through in order to achieve that. You accepted it as part of the norm. You weren't just pulled in and then told that all this would happen to you. You were told what was expected of you as you went along in your training. We were free to leave at any time we wanted to. There wasn't anyone forcing us to stay.'

Sister Margaret was happy to see the end of the old-fashioned habits and wimples and is enjoying her ministry in the community. But she mourns the passing of some of the old traditions. 'We had the old-fashioned clothing ceremonies which were lovely,' she says. 'There was a ritual in that and I don't think we should get rid of everything. There's a beautiful thing of leaving one part of life and moving on to the next. We need beauty. We need tradition. I'm not talking about antiquated rules but we can learn a lot from tradition.

'That's why I'm pleased about the resurgence in English spirituality. For years they never bothered about it. And I think for English children that's their culture, that's what they have to be trained in, just as I was trained in my Celtic spirituality. We never put a name to it, it was part and parcel of everyday life. I'm glad to see people researching the English saints and the English spirituality and mysticism. Because I don't think we must ever lose tradition. We must never lose that heritage.'

Sister Margaret's present lifestyle shows how much religious life has changed over the last 30 years. She was a teacher by the time the Holy Family sisters simplified their dress and reverted to their baptismal names and she remembers the squeals of delight from pupils who didn't realize that nuns had legs. 'It was a result of Vatican II that we researched our archives and discovered that our founder never wanted us to have a habit,' she says. 'He wanted us to be like other people and and live like them, catering for the needs of the area. For hygiene purposes I would say our modern dress is far healthier.'

With that change in philosophy, to say nothing of the drop in the number of young women wanting to join the teaching and nursing orders, Sister Margaret's convent in the Sparrow Hall district of Liverpool was becoming too big for the remaining sisters. The order decided to put the building to more general use. Sister Margaret was asked to stay in the area by moving into a flat and she admits she was frightened at first. For half a century she had never had to worry about paying bills and she certainly had no idea how to budget for them.

'People used to tell me that all the bills came in January and February and that was an awful time,' she says. 'I just didn't understand what they were going on about – but now I know. The first month I was desperate. I had to get food in, I had to pay bills. I was wondering which bill to pay first.'

Five years on, the experience has made Sister Margaret much more aware of the lives of the people she is working with. 'They show me the greatest respect,' she says. 'They would treat me differently if I had a habit on. I know the struggles they have with finances and with relationships. They are very open. There are some people around here who are in the lower income bracket and they are finding it a struggle to make ends meet but it's marvellous how they do it.

'If you're unemployed and living on income support or family credit, you've still got to give your children what everybody else is having or they are going to be labelled. And no mother – I'm speaking as a woman here – no mother will allow her children to be labelled.'

As press officer for the Association of British Contemplatives, Redemptoristine Sister Mary Bernadette has the job of answering many press enquiries 'and getting all the brickbats'. She's been dubbed 'the media nun' and has been compared to PR guru Lynn Franks. In fact, in 1996 the two women teamed up for a special edition of Radio 4's *Woman's Hour*.

Sister Mary Bernadette's job is to make the life of contemplative nuns and monks – those whose basic job is to pray – better known. She says that the enquiries she now receives show a rising interest in all things spiritual. 'There's a definite interest in spirituality these days,' she says. 'You can see that from the number of books that are being produced on prayer. They're obviously selling, otherwise publishers wouldn't publish them. People seem to want to get in touch with the unknown. They don't know it's God, but they want to get in touch with somebody.'

Sister Mary Bernadette reports that her own order has seen a rise in the number of young women expressing an interest in their way of life. 'Most convents have had more enquiries,' she says. 'They haven't always materialized, but we do get the enquiries. They mostly come from people in their mid-thirties, which is good because they know what they're leaving and they have something to offer.'

She stresses that the life of an enclosed nun these days is a world away from Audrey Hepburn's experiences in *The Nun's Story*. 'Life has changed,' she says. 'The way we treat our postulants is quite different to the way we were treated. We would want someone who is pretty mature, or as mature as people can be. We are looking for women of deep faith because we don't always see the results of our prayer. They need to have a sense of humour as it helps over difficulties in the religious life. We don't want them to be superwomen but it helps if they are.'

The nature of an enclosed community means that the life of the nuns is little known outside the convent walls. A journalist seeking entry needs canonical permission even for – perhaps especially for – an interview for a book like this. But such permission can be granted and to be shown around such a religious house is rather like peeping into the Secret Garden or being given a glimpse through the wardrobe into the land of Narnia.

Those sisters who are usually only seen praying – and then, only through the grille that separates the public and private parts of their chapel – live quite amazing lives on the other side of the enclosure. True, they are in the chapel several times each day, and during the night, but the rest of the time they don their aprons and get down to the practical tasks, including working the land to grow their own food and making items for sale. Anything that can be home made *is* home made.

The Poor Clares of Hawarden in North Wales have created everything themselves, from the embroidered crucifix to the altar made from a tree that fell in their garden. And Mother Teresa, novice mistress of the convent, says the sisters only bring in paid help when it is really necessary.

'If you're poor you have to be inventive,' she explains. 'If we can make it ourselves then we do. If we really can't cope with something we get someone in to do it for us – but we have to be driven.'

Like many other enclosed orders, the Hawarden nuns are experiencing something of a second spring. But few of the sisters, aged between 26 and 64, come from Christian backgrounds and most are converts to Catholicism. The present community includes an ex-hippy, an ex-biker and an ex-punk.

Mother Teresa, who began religious life in an active order, says that the religious orders are missing an age group, roughly that of the Vatican II years. 'There's a huge age gap in most orders,' she says. 'There is a lost generation. We were too young, too immature to take this great step in our stride and too old to profit from the reformation and it was very difficult.

'I went out once in two years for a very important general election. Then came the prophetic event called Vatican II of which we expected so much – and yet many hopes died simply because people didn't enter into the spirit of it. It was the same old story of religion almost against God, almost divorcing it from God, and God is a dynamic God.'

Sister Maria – she's the ex-hippy – believes that the religious congregations must constantly take a mirror to themselves and ask if they are being true to their calling. 'Many congregations are disappearing because they have ceased to be a sincere, legitimate witness to the Gospel and God does not prosper it,' she says. 'Where the Gospel is lived Christ is present. For us, the thing that matters, the thing that runs through us, is "is this life faithful to the Gospel?" And if it isn't we can't expect God to bless it by encouraging anybody else to live it.

'Periodically people turn up who have an illusion about themselves and about religious life which is unsustainable. They think it's a better choice, they think they're going up the social and mystical ladder. Sooner or later – generally rather soon – they find their way back to the front door and go and look for another life. Because that's exactly what this isn't.'

Or, as Mother Teresa puts it, 'If you're not in love, everything begins to grate on you.'

Just as the Hawarden nuns are mostly people who did not come from Catholic homes, so the number of priests in England & Wales has been boosted in recent years by convert clergymen. But the acceptance of so many married men for ordination as Catholic priests has also raised the question of those men who had given up their priesthood for love. Would they not now be allowed to return to their ministry? It was, said Archbishop Cormac, a 'sensitive' issue, but these ordinations were an exception that would not become the rule:

> They may feel hurt by this inclusion in the priesthood of those who are married while they themselves are excluded from its ministry. While acknowledging these feelings, it is important to note that the two situations are not quite the same. One involves those who gave the solemn undertaking of lifelong celibacy, the other does not.

What is being permitted now is in response to a
personal journey of faith from a Church which permitted
the marriage of its clergy. The Catholic tradition has not
included such a permission. Even the Orthodox tradition
permits such marriages, but only before ordination and
never after that irrevocable step has been taken. At this
time it is important that we are sensitive to those who
feel so excluded, while encouraging them to continue in
their life of faith and service, as the disciplines and prac-
tices of the Church permit.

The tradition of a celibate clergy is just that, a Church tradition.
Unlike the ordination of women, it is not considered a theological issue and, in theory, Pope John Paul could end compulsory
celibacy tomorrow. There have always been voices calling for
discussion about the issue of celibacy and, given some of the cases
of lovelorn priests quitting the cloth in the last few years, some of
those voices have become louder.

✝

8. This Troublesome Priest

At the turn of the last century, Canon James Keatinge of Southwark warned his fellow clergy that

> from the beginning, men and women have been a danger to each other, and clergy on account of their obligation of perpetual celibacy are bound in an especial way to take the precautions needful in presence of this danger. The danger on either side seldom comes from malice – its beginnings are in weakness and frailty of human nature and then we drift.

The good Canon went on to advise priests to 'keep the women about us in their place by keeping ours' and warned the 'tired' priest with time on his hands from 'finding his way to the kitchen' where 'he is always welcome', for 'he will pay for it'.

Quite what dangers were lurking behind the pantry door Canon Keatinge doesn't really say, but he does go on to recommend safety in numbers and advises that 'two women in your house are better than one', adding that 'if you are to take your recreation with women or girls, you will do less harm if you are with a dozen at a time than with one'.

Nearly a century later Archbishop Cormac said that such advice was not quite as old-fashioned as it sounds: 'In the old days priests were more protected,' he said. 'Now they are asked to be totally available in a very free society. They are vulnerable and the seminaries need to train them how to express their love for people with certain safeguards.'

Speaking after the resignation of Roddy Wright, the bishop of Argyll and the Isles who had entered into a relationship with a 40-year-old divorcée, Cardinal Basil Hume delivered a passionate defence of the benefits of priestly celibacy. He admitted, however, that some 'excellent' people were being lost to the ministry because they could not live the celibate life:

> I am not advocating any change in the law. I believe celibacy is the right answer for the Church. It brings important value and in a society which is obsessed with sex it serves as a fine witness to love. It is a value we have to preserve.
>
> Celibacy is always difficult and in many ways it is painful every day. But it is naïve to think that married life is any easier. For both married men and celibates, it is a challenge to stick to the vows they have made. But we have to be endlessly understanding and compassionate to those who fail to live up to the ideal. Human life is complex and we all carry within us our fallen natures.
>
> It is Church law that priests should be celibate, not divine law, and so can be changed by the Pope in thirty seconds. But I think only when the opinion has changed worldwide would the Pope consider changing the ruling.

Less than three days after the Cardinal's statement it was revealed that a Northamptonshire woman had two daughters through her affair with a local priest. He visited his 'family' regularly but refused to give up his priesthood, which, he said, was for life. However, his order had suspended him when the second child's imminent arrival was announced.

In January 1997 Father John Clarke told his parishioners at Our Lady of Lourdes Church, Haworth, that he had offered his resignation to his bishop after falling in love but did not have 'marriage in view'. And in July the following year Dominican

Father Paul Parvis, 52, announced his intention to marry a former student – who was also a former nun. Later that year Father Patrick 'PJ' Morrissey resigned his post to live with a married woman and their three-year-old son, saying 'people don't realize how lonely it is to be a priest'.

And in December 1999 Father Francis Meehan moved Laura O'Shea and her four children into his Manchester presbytery, having been preparing her for marriage to her boyfriend, the children's father. Facing the gaggle of reporters who had gathered outside, Father Meehan maintained there was 'no scandal to report' and if there was 'we would have run off long ago'. He insisted that his decision to quit the priesthood had come first and he had later asked Laura whether she and the children would be willing to come with him. The *Manchester Evening News* certainly considered this was enough of a 'scandal' and splashed 'Priest quits in love row' across its front page that night. By the following morning every paper in the country had run the story. The children's father said he felt 'OK' about it and wished his former fiancée well.

Nobody can see inside the heads of these priests. Most appear, quite simply, to have fallen in love. But there is no evidence that relaxing the celibacy laws would make any difference to the number of clergy scandals that reach the national headlines. Father Michael Gaine, a member of the Movement for a Married Clergy (MMaC), formerly the Movement for the Ordination of Married Men, believes it wouldn't solve problems but create different ones.

'What we would have then would be divorced priests,' he says. 'We would have priests refusing to send their children to local Catholic schools because other schools had a better academic tradition. I want married men to be considered as eligible for ordination to priesthood as celibate men. There isn't a convincing theological argument for not ordaining married men.'

Father Gaine believes that ordaining married men wouldn't necessarily solve the problem of the shortage of priests and he cites the Anglican and Free Churches, which are also suffering a decline in the number of clergy. But, he stresses, it isn't the statistics that matter. 'That's the wrong argument,' he says. 'If we're going to have married clergy it must be for a theological reason. My reason is that marriage and ordination are two great sacraments and they can be compatible with each other. The present Pope has said it is not a question of fundamental natural law that priests are celibate, it's just appropriate that it should be so. We would still have priests who would opt for celibacy as you have explicitly celibate Anglican clergy who choose celibacy as a way of life – and then it is a real witness because it is freely chosen.'

Now approaching his seventieth birthday and contemplating retirement, Father Gaine, who has never expressed any desire to be married himself, admits things have changed over the last half-century. 'In my time we wanted to be priests and we accepted the fact that the price we paid for that was to make a commitment to celibacy,' he says. 'But we didn't *choose* celibacy – it was accepted as a part of the package, part of the definition of priesthood.'

According to a 1996 survey in *The Catholic Herald*, three-quarters of English Catholics believed priests should be allowed to marry and the majority believed that the celibacy laws would be changed 'eventually', a move that would be good for the Church.

The following year the Bishops' Conference admitted there was a problem when they set up a team to look into the best ways to help women who had had affairs with priests. Bishop Christopher Budd told Radio 4's *Today* programme: 'If a priest has fathered a child by a woman, in some ways he is personally responsible and that means he may have to leave the ministry and earn sufficient to support the child and the mother. Where you have relationships which are clandestine and somebody is still in the priestly ministry, the truth must come out and the priest concerned must accept that truth, must move out of the ministry and do what he can to support either the woman or the woman and children.'

For every priest who makes a dramatic announcement to the newspapers that he is quitting his collar for love, there appear to be two more who are wrongly accused of sowing their wild oats.

There's quite a bit of cash in 'kiss-and-tell' tales. Catholic priests are just as easy targets as cash-conscious Conservatives, lovelorn Liberals and over-sexed Socialists, and the results can be just as damaging.

Writing in the late 19th century, Cardinal Edward Henry Manning advised priests to suffer false accusations as 'our Divine Master' suffered them and to be sure that 'innocence, suffering under sin, suffers for sinners'. Nobody would deny that the great Manning was offering substantial spiritual comfort to those who found themselves in the occasional tricky situation. But he was writing at a time when the mass media, while not bound by the current libel laws, didn't have the penetration it has today. What advice would he have given to the priest who won a 1999 libel action against the *Sun* but soon found that, while he might have earned a few quid, he had lost his previously untarnished name?

Cardiff's 70-year-old archbishop, John Aloysius Ward, was falsely accused in January 1999. Not just accused, in fact, but visited by the police and arrested. The accusations of sexual abuse against a seven-year-old girl almost 40 years earlier had been made through – believe it or not – the *News of the World*. While protesting his innocence, Archbishop Ward cancelled all his public engagements and published a statement:

> On Saturday 16 January 1999, I was contacted by the *News of the World* newspaper. They had received information that allegations of sexual abuse of a seven-year-old child had been made against me. These dated back to 1960/61. Who released this information is not yet known, but it is part of the kind of abuse which is turned on the accused, innocent or guilty.
>
> No one is above the law. Accusation must be answered in an atmosphere of trust that upholds the principle that a person is innocent until proven guilty. This is not possible when police connections with the media precede arrest and the interview which follows. This is not the practice of most police authorities but it is common enough. Tragically, there have been cases where priests

have been guilty of heinous crimes which must be condemned, but many priests have been falsely accused and, because of police connections with the media, their lives have been made a misery and their ministry damaged. The Church has had enough of these tragedies and travesties of injustice and abuse.

In the present climate, none of us is safe from false accusations. Now that a bishop is so accused, I will use my position to go public and ask the kind of questions that challenge present procedures that are a dangerous machinery for grave miscarriages of justice.

I have not been charged, only interviewed. I expect the process to be concluded in the near future. I vigorously deny these allegations against me. The truth will out. It will set us free. And those who know me will have no problem accepting that.

Less than three months later Archbishop Ward had been cleared of all allegations and he thanked all those who had believed in his innocence:

I am pleased that the allegations are seen to be without foundation. I was never charged and I have always vigorously protested my innocence. I would like to express my thanks to all those who have supported me with their prayers at this difficult time.

One such supporter was Monsignor Michael Buckley, agony uncle of *The Universe* newspaper and himself the subject of allegations of sexual misconduct. He says he felt a 'tremendous feeling of abandonment by the powers-that-be that should have helped me'. Although he still continues with his healing ministry all over the country, he says he has to keep his head down.

'Whenever the press or the media talk about me in any context, they will mention that,' he says. 'Even though I've carried on with no regrets, it has made me keep my head below the parapet. But, at the same time, it made me aware that I had to reach out to people in a similar situation. Ever since I've heard of it happening to anybody I've immediately said, "My God, I know what this fella's going through." It's opened my healing ministry in a way that, without that horrible experience, I couldn't have.'

For one priest, false accusations proved the breaking point. Father Benjamin O'Sullivan, a monk of Ampleforth Abbey, killed himself in 1996 while being investigated by – are you ready for this? – the *News of the World*. The paper had set up a meeting between the monk and a 22-year-old gay man at London's Dorchester Hotel. The man quizzed Father Benjamin about the boys at Ampleforth College and steered the conversation around to whether or not the 34-year-old monk fancied any of them. Outside, photographers using long-range cameras snapped the two men as they left. Not knowing what was happening, Father Benjamin returned to his abbey where he was met by a reporter who wished to talk to him about alleged paedophile activities.

Father Benjamin asked for half an hour alone to think about how best to answer the accusations. While the reporter waited, he took a plastic bag into the Abbey grounds and suffocated himself. His body was found the next morning and a note in his habit declared his innocence: 'I never did anything wrong as they accused me. May God forgive them and have mercy on my soul.'

After recording a verdict of suicide, coroner Michael Oakley described the *News of the World*'s behaviour as 'underhand and despicable'. Father Benjamin was mentally fragile, he added, and the newspaper's investigation had proved to be 'the last straw'.

The paper's allegations proved to be false. Father Benjamin had never been under any suspicion of improper behaviour towards any of the boys at Ampleforth College. He had, however, seen at first hand how such allegations can affect a religious, as one of his brother monks was being investigated at the time. The previous autumn another monk at Ampleforth had been suspended from all school activities after he admitted touching a sleeping boy in an 'inappropriate' manner in the early hours of the morning. He admitted indecent assault at a magistrate's court hearing in April 1996.

At least this man admitted the folly of his 'inappropriate' actions and is now spending time away from Ampleforth undergoing rehabilitation. But, as one former monk from a different congregation explains: 'It's been going on for so long in some places that in the past it has been quite acceptable with certain communities. A boy who has given or received sexual favours from a teacher and then goes on to become a monk himself, thinks nothing of passing on the tradition. Some priests presume that all lads share their own high sex drive and almost think they are doing the victim a favour – they see it as a bit of laddish horseplay. Thankfully, these days, youngsters can speak out.'

During the 1990s, the papers were full of child abuse cases involving Catholic priests and religious. The Irish Church received a particular battering that caused the Christian Brothers to issue a public apology for any abuse connected with their order. American dioceses began insuring themselves against the growing claims for compensation and in Britain the dioceses announced child protection policies to safeguard both youngsters and those working with them.

In Clifton diocese Bishop Mervyn Alexander brought in his own child protection team after police dropped all charges against one of his priests who had been accused of sexually abusing boys. The priest admitted his offences and voluntarily underwent psychiatric investigation. Bishop Alexander issued a statement saying: 'We understand that [he] admitted sexual offences quite incompatible with his ministry. He also admitted an offence in a letter to the family of one of the victims'.

Other priests who have admitted that their behaviour was far from proper have found themselves in prison just like any other child abuser. In 1996 Father Adrian McLeish of Gilesgate, Durham, was sentenced to six years for abusing boys aged 10 to 18 and exchanging pornographic material on the internet. Police found that McLeish, 45, had stored nearly 9,000 pornographic images – including many of children – and his case was thought to be the first that proved a direct link between child abuse and internet porn.

Summing up, Mr Justice Moses told McLeish: 'For six years you sexually abused four young boys, some of whom you groomed with a view to indulging your future desire. You had a vast collection of child pornography and, in four months, you spent 143 hours building up your collection. It is difficult to stop such distribution of these pictures. Users are rarely caught but it is the active part you have played in the distribution of these pictures which is the real crime. It is also clear you lived up to your fantasies, fuelled by pornography to which you had access through the internet.'

Two years later Father Eric Taylor, 78, was jailed for seven years for abusing boys in his care at the Father Hudson Society's home in Warwickshire between 1957 and 1965. The court heard that the priest had then stood by and watched the boys beaten by nuns when they tried to complain about their ordeals. Judge Marten Coates described Taylor as 'a disgrace to your cloth and the Church you proclaim'. He said that only Taylor's age had saved him from a much longer sentence.

For Father John Lloyd the sentence didn't stop at the eight-year prison term imposed by Cardiff Crown Court in February 1998. Later that year the 57-year-old was also officially dismissed from the clerical state by a decree from the Congregation for Clergy, the first time such an action has been taken against a priest in Britain for several centuries.

Such cases have a knock-on effect and can often leave other priests feeling demoralized. 'It leaves clergy feeling vulnerable because it creates all sorts of new approaches,' explains a priest from Cardiff Archdiocese. 'Up to now people could come to the door and you didn't mind talking to people across the whole age range, they could float into the house and out again. Now you can't let a teenager, or younger, come into the house because any allegation can be made. This used to be a reasonably open house but now one has to be very careful.'

The Cardiff priest says that people outside the Church are generally 'very sympathetic' and understand that 'there are bad eggs in all sorts of professions'. But when one person commits offences such as these the Catholic community in general feels the hurt. 'The whole body suffers. You come through different phases, just like bereavement. First you come through denial and you can be deafened by the silence as people are not prepared to talk about it. Then there's an overflow of emotion as people do want to talk about it.

'We have to talk and bring it to the surface. When it's down in the gut the suspicion is that there are others around. When it comes to the surface a lot more sense comes out.

'People can feel demoralized but we have to counter that. As priests we have a message to give. We have a faith which is very inspiring and very helpful to people. We have to believe in our faith. There are many priests out there who are doing a very good job and many Catholics who are very supportive, who believe in what we're doing.' He adds that the Church authorities must be seen to be following the same guidelines as schools and social services and that priests and lay workers must all get used to working under new procedures.

Portsmouth diocese took the initiative in June 1993 when they issued guidelines advising parishes how best to deal with allegations of child abuse by clergy: 'If an allegation is made to anyone that a child has been sexually abused by a priest or Church personnel then the allegation must immediately be referred to the local Social Services Office, and the chairman of the Standing Committee on Sexual Abuse.'

Following claims that some clergy had been known abusers and were protected by their bishops, the Portsmouth Standing Committee wanted to make it clear that the welfare of the child was to be paramount and that they did not want to appear to be putting the priest concerned first. 'Under no circumstances should the alleged perpetrator be informed or interviewed,' continued the guidelines. 'This is for the protection of the victim and to prevent the perpetrator exerting pressure on the victim or the victim's family.' If a criminal investigation was launched, priests and employees would be suspended on full pay. While they would be offered accommodation, counselling and treatment, any future employment would be 'restricted'.

The following year the bishops of England & Wales published *Child Abuse: Pastoral and Procedural Guidelines*, which reaffirmed the Church's belief in 'the dignity of children' and stressed that 'all child abuse includes a betrayal of trust' which is compounded when 'a person is presumed to act according to certain moral standards'. Abuse by a priest, it says,

> is a terrible contradiction since symbolically and sacramentally he makes present the redemptive mediation of Christ. Child abuse committed by a priest arouses a mixture of shock, disbelief, outrage, shame, betrayal and many other emotions which can be fully expressed only by those who have been victims themselves or have been close to them.

The 36-page document lays down procedures similar to those of the Portsmouth model. It recommends that each diocese should appoint a 'person of mature pastoral judgement' to represent the bishop in child abuse cases, stating that 'preliminary investigation must be circumspect'. Church authorities are told to 'make every effort to support the police and others who are working to establish the truth' and if a priest is found guilty of abuse 'it is presumed that normal pastoral practice will be provided throughout this period whether the guilty party is in prison or on probation. The timing of any ecclesiastical procedures will be adjusted to the requirements of criminal penalties'. As in the Portsmouth recommendations, 'the protection of children is the priority' and 'in the case of a cleric being found guilty of abuse, the question of his future as an officiating pastor must be faced' with counselling, therapy and spiritual renewal preceding 'any consideration of a return to the ministry'.

Much of the bishops' child abuse document concerns the treatment of abusers but *Healing the Wound*, a set of guidelines published two years later, redresses the balance by looking at how the Church can 'best offer care and support in the matter of child sexual abuse'. In 1995 the Catholic Youth Service (CYS) had already published *From Guidelines to Good Practice*,

intended to protect both children and youth workers from actual
or alleged abuse:

> The child-orientated values of our parishes tend to make
> us assume that every member of the community is of the
> same mind and we therefore expect that everybody is
> trustworthy. Research has shown that the diocesan faith
> community provides the paedophile with a close family
> environment in which it is easy to operate. As a diocesan
> family we must come to a deep understanding of all the
> facets of this situation and commit ourselves to safeguard
> the well-being of our children and young people.

While the bishops of England & Wales were publishing *Healing
the Wound*, the bishops of Australia published an apology to all
victims of clergy sexual abuse. Many of these youngsters were
British orphans who had been shipped out to the continent as part
of a government scheme to give them a new start. Some found
themselves little more than slave labourers to the religious orders
who were building new schools and others were regularly abused
with no hope of having their complaints believed or even heard.

In fact the Australian bishops almost went too far in their
attempt to be seen as above criticism. They sought to ban their
priests from having any private contact with children and there
was even a suggestion that confessionals should have glass
viewing panels so the youngsters could be seen if not heard. 'It
is designed to increase our accountability to the community,'
Father David Cappo explained to the *Daily Telegraph*, 'and to
give clear signals that we have taken a whole range of complaints
about sexual abuse very seriously.'

In 1999 the Catholic Church in Scotland issued pocket-sized
guides for priests and church workers, warning against 'inappropriate physical or verbal contact', and launched a phone line for
children who were being abused. The scheme came under criticism from Action Against False Accusations of Abuse (AAFAA)
who claimed it placed priests in a vulnerable position and made
them targets for trumped-up allegations that, even if disproved,

could ruin a priest's life. Monsignor Tom Connelly, spokesman for the Church in Scotland, accepted that there were problems but said the protection of children was paramount.

There is little more the Church can do to prevent cases of abuse and be seen to disapprove of any form of the crime. There will probably always be scandals of this sort but, hopefully, the issue now has such a high profile that abusers will not get away with prolonged campaigns. This is not without cost. As Monsignor Michael Buckley points out, priests, counsellors and teachers can no longer risk any sort of physical contact with children.

'I'm a very tactile person. I used to love to play with the kids after Mass,' he says. 'Priests may be celibate but they have a normal fatherly nature and these kids are the kids we've never had. But there's a tremendous apprehension when you pick a child up or touch them. There's the horrible feeling that you're looking around to see who's pointing the finger.

'The whole issue has had to be brought out but not the way it's been exploited. I feel it's been done in a vengeful, negative way, instead of being done as a positive thing, acknowledging that our society's gone wrong and that we need to put it right.'

In March 1999 Arundel & Brighton joined with the neighbouring dioceses of Southwark and Portsmouth to develop a common policy for child protection procedures in their dioceses. Archbishop Cormac said at the time:

> Experience has shown that the Church is often an open target for those with a paedophile tendency, and that the protection of the children entrusted to the care of our parish communities must have maximum priority. It is our responsibility to ensure that our parishes are safe communities for children. This can only be achieved by raising awareness of good practice in our parish communities in regard to child protection.
>
> There is a very great need for all of us who are engaged in pastoral activity involving children to implement what constitutes 'good practice' in our various ministries. It is now time to demonstrate a partnership of

priests, deacons, pastoral assistants, parish sisters and lay people working together to implement safe practice to safeguard our children – and adults who work with them.

Sex sells newspapers. Sex involving priests, nuns or vicars sells twice as many newspapers. Over the last few years there have been a few small news items about clergy committing other misdemeanours – including the priest convicted of drink-driving after consuming too much altar wine at Mass and the priest convicted of 'borrowing' £130,000 from church funds who had to be tracked down by Interpol – but it is the clergy child abusers who grab the headlines. While the number of clerical offenders represents just a tiny percentage, their actions overshadow the good work of the vast majority of priests going about their everyday ministry.

As Monsignor Michael Buckley points out, there has been some breakdown of trust between priests and people. And it will take time, and the many safeguards now being implemented, for that trust to be built up again. The Catholic Communication Centre's 1998 survey revealed that young people in particular are disillusioned by such scandals. As one said: 'I hear about Catholic priests having affairs with women or young boys when they are telling us to live such a righteous life. They are being hypocrites, aren't they?'

9. Lofty Conversions

When, in November 1999, Cherie Blair announced she was to become a mother for the fourth time there was great rejoicing – and not a little sniggering – throughout the land. This seemingly caring woman, who in many ways had taken on the mantle of Princess Diana, was obviously thrilled at her news and oblivious to comments that at least there was something her husband was good at.

The fact that she was also a Catholic prompted the Union of Catholic Mothers to suggest she was qualified to join them. It was at the time that Mrs Blair was complaining about the increasing amount of money she was having to spend on clothes for public engagements and the UCM thought they might be able help.

'I don't know why she doesn't join us,' said media officer Margaret McNicholas. 'She wouldn't have to worry about her wardrobe. We hand down things like maternity dresses because you never get the full wear out of them. That's what the UCM is all about – mothers, motherhood, bringing up children and getting the best for them. I know she seems to have such a full programme and to be such a busy lady, but having said that it's usually the busy ladies that find time to do more.'

It was all a touch tongue in cheek. But it was the UCM's way of thanking Cherie for being a good role model, for carrying a child that another middle-aged career woman might have considered an inconvenience.

'Cherie has two high-profile jobs and the child is still accepted and wanted,' says Mrs McNicholas. 'Many a parent in that situation would say they already had growing children, they had their career and they didn't want another child messing it up, so let's get rid of it.'

Following her husband's entry into Number Ten, Cherie Blair soon became a Catholic pin-up. She was a highly qualified woman from a Catholic background who was still practising her religion and ensuring her children went to Catholic schools – even if they were selective schools – and dragging her husband along too. Apart from Harold Macmillan and his flirtation with the idea of conversion to Catholicism, never had any Catholic been quite so close to the seat of power. On the Sunday following the general election, the Blairs were photographed going to Mass at Immaculate Heart of Mary Church, Great Missenden, four miles further from their new country home at Chequers than the parish church used by previous prime ministers.

Father John Caden, the Blairs' parish priest at their home constituency, is not at all surprised that Cherie has become a role model for Catholic womanhood. Father Caden, who has known the couple since 1982 and has partnered Tony on the tennis court, says: 'In the early days Cherie was very much the little mother at the back of the church with the children – it was Tony who used to do the readings – but I've heard her speak in her own right and she is a very capable woman.'

Here Father Caden has hit on what, for some, is a knotty problem. Tony Blair, the Queen's first minister, spends quite a bit of time in Catholic churches – far too much for the leader of a nation that is nominally Anglican. He went so far as to receive Communion, both in his Islington home parish of St Joan of Arc and while on holiday in Tuscany, an action that brought down criticism from Catholics and non-Catholics alike. It wasn't long before Cherie was accused of 'leading' the Prime Minister to Rome. Soon came the shock-horror stories that not only was the PM tagging along to Sunday Mass with his Catholic family, he was actually slipping into Westminster Cathedral alone during the week.

A Downing Street spokesman was given the job of denying the charges. 'There should be certain parts of any public figure's life that should be allowed to remain private,' he said. 'Where the Prime Minister goes to church is a matter for him and for his family. He has only once attended Mass at the cathedral on his own and he is not converting to Catholicism.'

Eventually the PM spoke up for himself and said his attendance at a Catholic church was simply a question of family tradition. 'People should not take it as a matter of political significance. My wife is a Catholic and my kids are brought up as Catholics. I have gone to Mass with them for years because I believe it is important for a family to worship together. I would not want to go to an Anglican or Protestant church when my wife and kids go to a Catholic one.'

Then, lo and behold, a 1999 *Sunday Times* survey put Tony Blair at the top of a list of the nation's spiritual leaders. The poll asked 2,000 people in England and Wales who they thought provided the best moral and spiritual leadership in Britain. And Tony Blair beat Cardinal Hume, Archbishop Carey and the Chief Rabbi hands down.

Of course it is quite possible that Tony will become a Catholic at some stage. He certainly wouldn't be the first husband and father to adopt the religion of his wife and kids. Whether or not he would do so while in office, and therefore still responsible for the appointment of Anglican bishops, is quite a different question.

His 1997 general election win certainly raised hopes of a new style of administration and Archbishop Cormac welcomed TV news coverage of the Blair family moving into Downing Street. It was, he said, 'a most moving image. It was a simple sign of the place of the family and of the right priorities for the future of our countries. As such it was a sign of hope.'

At the end of September 1850, Nicholas Wiseman returned from Rome wearing a cardinal's hat and waving the papal documents that confirmed the restoration of the hierarchy in England & Wales. Queen Victoria is said to have screeched, 'Am I Queen of England or am I not!' And when, 40 years later, she spied the cupola of the new Westminster Cathedral rising above the trees, she fumed, 'Who gave them permission to build it?' For a lady who was Supreme Governor of the Church of England – which she considered far too popish, preferring the Presbyterianism of Scotland – this was all too much.

Doubtless the old queen would have been far from amused when, a century later, her own great-great-granddaughter, Queen Elizabeth II, entertained Pope John Paul II inside Victoria's former home, Buckingham Palace. She would have been apoplectic to hear her descendant refer to Basil Hume as 'my Cardinal'. And she would probably have burst out of her over-tight corsets had she seen Queen Elizabeth enter Westminster Cathedral for Vespers. Not that the Queen's attendance at one of the cathedral's centenary services went unnoticed. Outside the building she was greeted with cries of 'No Popery', 'Betrayal' and 'The Pope is the Anti-Christ'. Inside she was greeted with applause as she took her seat before the high altar. Her presence was, said Cardinal Hume in his homily, 'a further affirmation of the place that we Catholics have in the nation'.

Things have certainly changed since Victoria's time. When she came to the throne Catholics were only just being legally emancipated. During her reign, following the restoration of the hierarchy, many of the present dioceses were formed and their cathedrals built. These days the only prohibition on Catholicism is the 1701 Act of Settlement that bans Catholics from the throne or from marrying the monarch. Recent attempts to have the 300-year-old law abolished have been resisted. Even the Prime Minister, with his increasingly Catholic CV, is against changing the law as it would involve redrafting too many pieces of legislation.

Speaking on BBC1 just after his own election had been announced, Archbishop Cormac said it was a question of freedom of religion: 'I think that, inasmuch as the Catholic community is part of this country, there is a strong part of me that would say that an heir to the crown should be free to marry whoever he wishes, whatever denomination, and there must be freedom here. I think that this is a question that needs to be looked at.'

Despite the protests outside Westminster Cathedral, being a Catholic is no longer seen as being disloyal to the monarchy as it was when the Act of Settlement was passed. And when, in 1993, the Duchess of Kent, a close relative of the Queen, became a Catholic there was little controversy. The *Catholic Times* celebrated the occasion with a front-page banner that read 'The Duchess of Kent – Welcome Home'. One or two bishops complained to the paper's editor that this was a touch 'triumphal'. 'Yes,' he proudly replied. 'It was.'

Of course, the Duchess of Kent wasn't the only public figure to have converted to Catholicism in recent years. Princess Diana's mother, Frances Shand-Kydd, not only became a Catholic but set about building a chapel on the holy isle of Iona, the first Catholic house of prayer on the island in centuries. And after her daughter's meeting with Mother Teresa there were rumours that Princess Diana would follow her mother to Rome.

Then there were public figures who had lost faith in what was happening in their own church, like Ann Widdecombe and John Gummer. There were celebrities like Richard Coles of the Communards and *The Big Breakfast*'s Johnny Vaughan, who insisted that his faith was a private matter but conceded that 'Yes, I am seeing a man about God.' At around the same time, comedian Harry Enfield said he was returning to the Church of his childhood and Boyzone's Ronan Keating announced he would remain a virgin until his marriage because of his religious beliefs. Liz Dawn – *Coronation Street*'s Vera Duckworth – hung a photograph of herself with Pope John Paul in her real-life Salford pub. Paul O'Grady, the man behind Lily Savage, revealed that he keeps a bottle of Lourdes water by his bed. Week by week throughout the late 1990s, the Catholic press revealed that yet another public figure was either flirting with Catholicism or returning to it. The faith of Italian waiters and Irish navvies had acquired a certain cachet and, all of a sudden, it was trendy to be Roman.

Catholic peer Lord Alton of Liverpool believes the Catholic Church has become attractive because it is offering a clear, constant message at a time of uncertainty. 'The Church has spoken with confidence, not least with the publication of things like *The Common Good'*, he says. 'The world itself has become incredibly confused, it has been looking for certainty from some quarter and the Church has been providing that in a firm but loving way. It's not shrill or harsh and that's important too.'

Ten years ago, Lord Alton was one of a group of people working in the Palace of Westminster who arranged for the regular celebration of Mass in the crypt chapel. He says the opportunity for various devotions, including Stations of the Cross in Lent, has been welcomed by many. 'People sometimes slip into those things who either you didn't know were Catholic or who are wanting to know more about the Church. That's been a big difference, that in this last decade there have been a number of very high-profile converts, people who have become interested in the Catholic Church.'

Franciscan priest Father Michael Seed has been in effect an unofficial chaplain to the House of Commons for several years. He began grabbing the headlines when it was revealed that he had been involved in helping many famous people on the journey that led them to Catholicism. Understandably he can't – and won't – comment on individual cases. But he refutes accusations of 'poaching' and says that people are freely seeking out the Catholic Church because of its clear teaching and its willingness to accept people wherever they are. In other words, it's the church for sinners or, as Father Seed puts it, 'it's the messiness which attracts a lot of people to Catholicism'.

'People are not perfect and they are trying to find a church for the non-perfect,' he says. 'From Adolf Hitler to Mother Teresa, the Catholic Church is a church for saints and sinners and it's very messy. That's the reason it will always attract people. And, of course, it is the essence of the Church. There is no such thing as denominations, there is only the Christian Church. Our duty is to be much more Christlike, rather than emphasizing our differences – to go back, as it were, to simply being Christians. But, whether we like it or not, we do have to have a source, so the papacy is to be seen as an enabling power, a servant power. At the end of the day Catholicism has no monopoly on spirituality or salvation.'

Father Seed himself converted to Catholicism nearly 25 years ago and says that 'the reason I became a Catholic and the reason I stay a Catholic are very different'.

'I became a Catholic because of all the dirtiness and sinfulness. The Catholic Church is able to cope with all that very well. The essence of the Catholic Church – its substance, its foundation – is that it's *the* Christian Church. That's what I believe in. It might shock people to hear me say this, but often I think to myself that my concern is not always with remaining a priest, but with putting up with the bumpiness and blunderliness of Catholicism itself. What I find difficult is staying a Catholic. I am much happier being a Franciscan with its great spirit of universal acceptance and its love of all created things.'

In June 1999 the Catholic bishops announced in a 2000-word document that they would be willing to take seats in a reformed House of Lords if so nominated, stressing that any elected places should be reserved for lay people. 'It is no part of the bishop's job to seek power,' they said. 'But at the same time there cannot be no-go areas for the Church.' There have been no Catholic bishops in the upper House since the Reformation, and canon law forbids them from taking up public office 'whenever it means sharing in the exercise of civil power'. Archbishop Cormac is said to be in consultation with the Vatican about the implications should he be invited to take up a seat. But the bishops have proposed that rather than Catholic representation in the House of Lords, they would prefer there to be a Catholic 'voice'. 'For if the House were to have members on behalf of the Church itself,' they say, 'they would not be there in a personal capacity but rather to give voice to the moral and spiritual teaching of the Catholic Church.'

The bishops of England & Wales have certainly not been shy of raising their own 'voice' on governmental issues in recent years. So much so that they have been accused of being party political, with a particular bias towards the Left. The bishops' 1997 pre-election document *The Common Good* advised Catholics to bear in mind the Church's social teaching and their own Christian responsibility when casting their votes.

'The main purpose of the document is long term and educational,' said Bishop David Konstant. 'It is to raise Catholics' knowledge and understanding of Catholic social teaching. This teaching is an indispensable part of the mission of the Church and is too little known. A second objective is to make a contribution to the national debate on the many subjects now being discussed because of the forthcoming general election. It is the Church's obligation to talk about the morality of legislation.'

If concern for the poor, the underprivileged and the marginalized can be interpreted as left wing, then *The Common Good* was definitely leaning towards socialism, hence accusations of bias from the right-wing press. Tory MP Ann Widdecombe, however, insisted that following Church teaching was bound to lead Catholic voters to the Right. 'All Catholics should take account of both biblical teaching and the teaching of the Catholic Church,' she told the *Daily Telegraph*, 'and that leads me to conclude that they should be voting Conservative.' And David Alton, then a Liberal Democrat MP, said voting Labour would be problematic for Catholics because of the party's policy on abortion.

Cardinal Hume picked up on the abortion issue in an interview with the same newspaper when he reiterated the Church's teaching that abortion was 'very evil and strikes at the bedrock of society', adding that 'if Catholics come across a candidate who is strongly or actively pro-abortionist, then they will not vote for them'.

The Cardinal insisted that he was not telling Catholics how to vote but warned them against becoming single-issue voters. 'Catholics have to vote according to their conscience,' he said. 'But I do say there are firm principles which have to be taken into consideration. I hope people will pay attention to my guiding principle, which is that all life is sacred and must be respected from conception to its natural end.' Those words, of course, could be seen as a shot across the bows of those so-called pro-lifers who vote against abortion but condone capital punishment and nuclear weapons.

Cardinal Hume spoke on social issues when, seven months after the Labour victory, he addressed the Catholic Agency for Social Concern. He presented the 'simple' concept of 'our common humanity' as vital to the governing of the country. 'So much, it seems to me, comes to just this,' he said. 'The more we can come to accept that each person matters, the stronger will be our sense of service.' He continued the same theme later that week when he urged the British Government to step up their lead in releasing third world countries from unpayable debt. He told Chancellor Gordon Brown that 'we have a duty to promote the common good' and that 'the universal common good demands that no nation should be left unaided because it is too poor or too much in debt'.

In September 1998 Bishop John Jukes told the Trades Union Congress that 'membership of a trade union should be presented as an opportunity to participate both in the search for justice and for success on the part of the enterprise as a whole'. The following year Cardinal Hume echoed Bishop Jukes's words when he urged Catholics to become 'active members' of a trade union as part of their Christian duty to serve the community.

In 1997 and 1998 the bishops of England & Wales called on the Government to develop a clearer strategy 'for harnessing international effort towards the goal of eventually eliminating nuclear weapons entirely'.

During their 1999 Low Week meeting the bishops issued statements covering just about every aspect of politics. They called on Catholics to participate more fully in public life; they called for an end to the war in the Balkans; they urged the United Nations to stop the 'cruelly damaging' sanctions on Iraq; they expressed their concerns about welfare rights contained in the Immigration and Asylum Bill; they welcomed the MacPherson report on the Stephen Lawrence inquiry with its claims of 'institutional racism'; and they repeated their call for an end to unpayable third world debt as part of the Jubilee Year 2000 celebrations. In short, having set out their agenda in *The Common Good*, the bishops were being seen to continue lobbying for a fairer, more Christian society. As Archbishop Cormac told a political gathering in Lewes in 1979:

the Church herself is a sign of something that transcends politics, namely a person's relationship with God ...

The Church cannot be bound to any political community, or any political system. Yet though the political community and the Church are distinct and independent of each other, they are linked because both are devoted to the personal and social vocation of mankind though under different titles.

Just as the Church 'cannot be bound' to any particular political philosophy, there is no political party whose philosophy can be aligned with Christian ideals. They all have policies that are diametrically opposed to Christian teaching and practice. Margaret Thatcher's famous denunciation of 'society' and Tony Blair's rejection of socialism mean that the Catholic Member of Parliament, whatever their party, must make compromises between their faith and their political allegiance.

Ann Widdecombe MP is one of those rare beasts, a politician with a conscience. She is on record as saying she feels guilty 'going home to warmth and comfort and passing people sleeping rough on a cold night'. She was educated at a Catholic convent school and, after years as a High Anglican and a period of agnosticism, she was received into the Catholic Church in 1993 having made it clear that she felt her former church's decision to ordain women was 'nonsense'. The Tory MP for Maidstone insists that she has no problems reconciling her religious beliefs with her party's policies.

'It very rarely happens that there is a conflict between my beliefs and the party's because most of those issues are free vote issues,' she says. 'Abortion, capital punishment, divorce law reform, homosexual age of consent, all that is always free vote territory. It's far more likely that you will get a conflict within the free vote territory.

'For example, when I was doing the Abortion Amendment Bill, it became very obvious that we weren't going to get our Bill unless we exempted unborn handicapped children from the 18-week limit. That, obviously, went against all our beliefs but, on the other hand, 92 per cent of all those aborted after the eighteenth week are not handicapped. Our view was that if you were faced with a shipwreck with 100 people on, you wouldn't let 100 people go down because you could only pull 92 off. So we decided to go ahead with that exemption against our own consciences. That's the sort of conflict you get.'

Miss Widdecombe says her Christianity is part of her make-up and therefore influences all aspects of her life, including her job: 'If you believe that God has to work through society, then he has to work through society's rulers, and that means there must be Christians in every major party.' She claims that on many issues, Catholics of all parties can stand united across party boundaries. 'On free vote issues it is accepted that it will be a cross-party affair,' she says. 'But the fact is that most pro-lifers, for example, are in the Tory party. There are a few in the Labour Party, but they are very few and they are subjected to enormous pressures.'

Many Tories certainly have an admirable voting record on the issues of abortion and euthanasia. But the moral high ground on all the other, equally important, life issues such as nuclear power, capital punishment, warfare and third world debt, lies more on the other side of the House of Commons. And when it comes to state support of those in financial need, all the major political parties have abandoned any moral approach as impractical, presumably because the necessary rise in taxation would not be considered politically expedient.

Lord Alton says that most politicians find themselves in a state of conflict at some time or another. It's a problem he calls 'the Thomas More clause'.

'Being an astute lawyer, More did all he could to avoid his ultimate confrontation with the king but in the end, to use his own words, he had to choose between being the king's servant or God's servant,' he explains. 'That is the dilemma that everyone will face in their own way and everyone has to cross their own Rubicons. They are not usually as dramatic as those that Thomas More had to face, but in their own small ways they will have to face those dilemmas.'

Lord Alton's own dilemma was certainly dramatic. As David Alton, MP for Liverpool Mossley Hill, he had become known for his battles to prevent expansion of the existing abortion law and to further limit its use in Britain. But at the 1992 Liberal Democrat conference in Harrogate, Mr Alton's party adopted a pro-abortion stance as policy. 'Having in the morning passed a resolution which provided for the welfare of goldfish on sale at amusement arcades and funfairs, in the afternoon they passed a resolution making abortion party policy for the first time,' he says.

When abortion was considered a matter of conscience, pro-lifers like Mr Alton had been able to exist in the same party as people like David Steele who had introduced the Abortion Act in 1967. With abortion now party policy, Mr Alton felt he could not stand for election as a Liberal Democrat again and, at the 1997 general election, he stood down as a Member of Parliament. He was, however, given a peerage by John Major and now sits in the House of Lords as an independent cross-bencher.

Lord Alton says he knows of many people 'who have not been selected as candidates or who have not been given preferment within their party because they refused to say politically correct things about abortion'. But he stresses that it is not just politicians who have qualms of conscience, citing several examples of scientists and health workers who have lost their jobs because of their pro-life beliefs.

Archbishop Cormac has certainly never been shy of speaking out on political issues. Less than a month before the 1997 general election he used a musical allusion to describe the Church's social teaching as 'a symphony, because it is built on very basic themes which are the foundation of all the other variations which develop from it'. In a pastoral letter read in all the churches of Arundel & Brighton Diocese, he said the values of the Gospel should be applied to 'the problems of our age and help all people to play an active part in building a just and compassionate society':

> The foundation of all Catholic social teaching is quite
> clearly the dignity of the human person. No other value

in our teaching has become so clear and apparent as the respect and honour that must be given to the human person at all stages from conception to natural death. How strange, that in our society where the rights of individuals are so publicly affirmed, the rights of the weakest and most vulnerable are increasingly ignored and denied. In particular, we should raise our voices in protest against the destruction of life in the womb and the casual manner in which our society has accepted the evil of abortion. No wonder that the Church is deeply involved in the pro-life movement and all policies that favour the advancement of persons so that they can live dignified lives.

Lord Alton says you cannot always presume that Catholic MPs will vote with you on what are seen as predominantly Catholic issues like abortion and euthanasia. 'It is true that in the 20th century the big issue that tended to sort people out has been the abortion question,' he says. 'But, when you get down to it, in 1967 for instance, only 31 people voted against the Abortion Act. Almost all of those were Catholic, but there were other Catholics who were not in the lobbies. It remains true today that, even on those touchstone issues, you can't be sure that all of your co-religionists will be there.'

In his pre-general election pastoral, Archbishop Cormac stressed that there was more than one issue facing Catholics in the polling booth. He stressed, too, the importance of maintaining an option for the poor, who 'have always had a special place in Catholic teaching'.

A brother of mine, who died some years ago, was a priest who, among his many other gifts, was a marvellous prison chaplain. He laughed with prisoners, helped their families, supported them in such a way that, even though everyone else seemed against them, they knew he was on their side. Because he was on their side they dared to hope that God was on their side. This, essentially, is what we mean when we talk about a preferential option for the poor. The poor, the marginalized, the prisoners, all those adrift in the community, are not a burden – they are our brothers and sisters with whom we share a common humanity.

He concluded the letter by reminding his flock of the need to keep a balance 'between the rights of the individual and the needs of society as such'.

A true flourishing of the individual will enhance the good of the whole community. Every individual has a duty to participate in promoting the welfare of the whole community. Indeed, there may come a point in a particular society where the gap between the very wealthy and those who are without begins to undermine the common good. Jesus in the Gospels repeatedly warns us about the dangers of over-attachment to material riches and that these dangers apply not only to the individual but to the community as a whole. We need to recognize, quite simply, that we are all responsible for one another.

The future of humanity does not depend on political decisions, however important they may seem at the time. Our future, as individuals and as a country, depends on a conversion of mind and heart to the will and the mind of God made manifest for us Christians in the presence and the teaching of our risen Lord.

Let's hope the Vatican does allow Archbishop Cormac to take up a seat in the House of Lords if one is offered. For he would be one of the few MPs promoting what he describes as 'policies that favour the advancement of persons so that they can live dignified lives'.

✠

Pilgrim Cormac

I began by saying that 'it's not much fun being Archbishop of Westminster'. Three months down the line I'd say that I wouldn't take on the job for a fistful of croziers, a dozen episcopal rings and a diamond-encrusted mitre. In the last few weeks I have listened to the arguments of liberals and traditionalists, left-wingers and right-wingers. I've spoken to people who mourn the passing of Benediction and those who would like to see the Catechism burned. And, I must admit, at times I've felt like cracking their heads together.

I'm still liberal enough to put up with the traditionalists, as long as they don't do it in the street and frighten the horses. But I no longer understand where they fit in. Groups like Pro Ecclesia et Pontifice do little to build up the Church community but tear into everyone else's efforts like so many vultures. They criticize bishops, priests, teachers, RE syllabuses and liturgical celebrations but their only contribution appears to have been reporting supposedly 'dissident' bishops to Rome. For 'dissident' read 'those who won't do what we want'.

If I was Pope – and I'm glad I'm not, as I don't think they can get *Emmerdale* in Vatican City – but if I was, I would tell those agitators of all hues to either shut up or get out. You are entitled to your views, but please stop telling the rest of us, bishops, priests and laity alike, that we have all got it dreadfully wrong.

It is time the public sparring came to an end. I will happily referee a final bout between the Association of Catholic Women and the Catholic Women's Network, or between Pro Ecclesia et Pontifice and We Are Church. My only condition is that a safety helmet must be provided.

My odyssey has taken me to cathedrals, convents, monasteries and schools. And it's helped me to realize where I am happiest – at a little old church up the road whose congregation is praying to survive the diocesan plans for reorganization.

Few of the people here can easily pay their gas and electric bills but they are giving their all to keep a roof on the parish hall. Most have no hope of affording a holiday but they support the weekly bingo that is raising money to send a handicapped child to Lourdes.

They don't care whether they sing to guitar or organ, whether it's ancient or modern, as long as it's a good tune and the words are meaningful. They don't mind whether they stand or kneel for Communion, as long as no one removes the altar rails that were funded by great-aunt Mary's sponsored walk across the Pennines.

Few turned up for the meeting to discuss the diocesan rationalization policy, but those with cars are queuing up to take the elderly people shopping on Saturday afternoon. They welcome remarried people and gay couples either unaware of, or not caring about, the Church's rules on sex outside marriage, but woe betide anyone who says the rosary is outdated or tries to remove their statue of the Sacred Heart. Tell them they need 'empowering' and they'll tell you to get lost.

They know nothing about 'the role of the laity' or 'collaborative ministry' but they do everything in their power to keep their church alive, to teach their children and to organize all the social activities that keep a parish going. And if all their efforts fail, and they are forced to surrender their crumbling old building, these are the people who will happily gather on the local canal bank to hear the words of a carpenter's son.

The good news? Sorry, I almost forgot. Well, in short, the majority of Catholics are getting along quite happily, thank you very much. They work with their priests, not against them. They don't report their bishops to the Vatican, because they are too fond of them and want to keep them. For most of these 'ordinary' Catholics, the arguments of progressives and traditionalists are just so many more words they could well do without.

Not only are the numbers of student priests and aspirant religious rising – slowly admittedly, but they are rising – the number of people taking part in retreats and other spiritual exercises is higher than ever before. The annual New Dawn Conference has drawn thousands of people to Walsingham over the last few years, to say nothing of the huge numbers of people who visit the Norfolk shrine on more traditional pilgrimages every week.

The percentage of our younger people who could be labelled 'practising' is not as high as some people would like. But take a look at the commitment of those who are. Thousands of youngsters from England & Wales volunteer to work with the sick and disabled at Lourdes every summer, and the emphasis here is definitely on 'work', as a trip to Lourdes is no picnic. Many hundreds more are involved with the Youth 2000 initiatives where they really do stand up and let themselves be counted. These are only two examples. There are countless youth events and celebrations taking place all over the country at any given moment.

Moreover, how do we interpret the number of practising Catholics living in 'irregular unions' like second marriages or same-sex relationships? Given the hard line of canon law these people might just have walked away, but the fact that they are still there is a testimony to the ministry of the many excellent priests working in parishes all over Britain.

When Nicholas Wiseman, the first Archbishop of Westminster, was enthroned in 1850, Catholicism was only just tolerated in Britain and its rites and rituals were often lampooned in magazines like *Punch*. A century and a half later, Catholic bishops are consulted by Government committees on all sorts of issues and back in March there were several temporal VIPs in Westminster Cathedral to witness the installation of Cormac Murphy-O'Connor, Wiseman's latest successor. This acceptance of Catholics by society at large is often attributed to the efforts of Cardinal Hume who, undoubtedly, had the necessary touch. But credit must also go to the way ordinary Catholics live their lives.

Before the Reformation, the Church provided massively for those in need. In the following centuries this work was taken on by the State. But since successive governments have eroded the welfare system, Catholics have stepped back into the breach. All those people give time and money without even thinking about it, to those in need.

'People stump up spontaneously,' says CAFOD's Judith Rees. 'We received £467,000 for Mozambique without asking. We hadn't sent out an appeal to people, it just happened. We always get a good response to emergencies, but the thing that struck me about Mozambique was the donations from the small parishes. There was one for £4,011 from a single small parish. It's a bad news story as far as Mozambique is concerned but it's a good news story as far as people's humanitarian reaction is concerned. And it's not just in the fundraising but in the campaigning as well. We had great support for the debt campaign.'

Then there are the vast amounts of money raised by groups like the Catholic Women's League, which funds hostels for the asylum seekers so loathed by the *Daily Mail*. That's without mentioning the work these women do to support children and old people and their commitments in the courts and prisons.

The St Vincent de Paul Society works tirelessly for people in need, providing furniture for those without and offering practical help for those no longer young enough to help themselves. They organize holidays for children and whole families who wouldn't otherwise get a break.

Similarly, the Union of Catholic Mothers, those ordinary mums in parishes up and down the country, raised £40,000 for education in the third world during 1999, simply from jumble sales and collecting money in jam jars.

'That has come from women who have a lot of commitments to themselves and their children,' explains UCM national president Sheilagh Preston. 'We are still very good at reacting in a crisis. Last year we collected £37,000 for the homeless, and that money was in addition to the time and effort put into doing other things like collecting clothes and goods and helping at shelters. Ask a busy person and they are always there, always willing to go the extra mile.'

Mrs Preston dismisses the prophecies of doom that have come from endless statistics about falling numbers. 'I am an optimist and I think that what God wants will come through in time. That doesn't mean we don't have to help it along its way when we can, because we do. But there will still be a Church. Maybe it might be slightly different and we'll have to accept that. But I don't believe it will all fade away. I can't believe that.'

No doubt Mrs Preston will have been cheered by Archbishop Cormac's words when, preaching during his Mass of Installation, he said:

> I have no time for prophets of gloom. I do not believe these are gloomy times for the Catholic Church in our country. When the skies are dark the light shines more brightly. For those who follow Jesus Christ, there is the assurance that in him, God has visited his people. Just as in Jesus Christ the people were healed and taught about the Kingdom of God and assured that their sins were forgiven and that God had a destiny for each and every one of them, so it is true for us today.

In the same homily, Archbishop Cormac recalled a visit to the Outer Hebrides where he saw a Celtic stone with the ancient inscription: *Pilgrim Cormac – He went beyond what was deemed possible.* The words reminded our present Pilgrim Cormac of his own journey through life and the work to which he is committed:

> I know the Church must always be reformed and that it is composed of saints and sinners. The Church has always been the heart of my soul, the model of my spiritual being. It is to Christ's Church that I give my loyalty and my love.

So I continue as a pilgrim traveller, always teaching, yes, but always listening and always looking for the road ahead. It is not for nothing I chose my motto *Gaudium et Spes* – Joy and Hope – and there will be much joy and much hope in the time ahead. I am not totally unlike that ancient Celtic traveller, the pilgrim who went beyond what was deemed possible.

The new Archbishop of Westminster has much ahead of him, but if he has one particular task it must surely be to reunite those discordant branches of the family of the Church in England & Wales. As he said the night before he officially took on his new assignment, we have no choice but to work together as a family:

It is a daunting task for me to confront this enormous challenge of endeavouring to be a shepherd, a pastor, to so many people. I cannot do it alone. I need you: priests, religious, lay people, to realize that it is together that we make up the Church of Jesus Christ and that it is together that we undertake this wonderful task of building up the Church in prayer, in liturgy, in community and in service to others. It is together that we become a sign to the world, a sign of truth and hope and love.

Happy travelling, Pilgrim Cormac.

✛

Bibliography

Butler, Carolyn, ed., *Faith, Hope and Chastity*, London: Fount, 1999

Carson, Michael, *Sucking Sherbet Lemons*, London: Victor Gollancz, 1988

Carson, Michael, *Yanking up the Yo-Yo*, London: Victor Gollancz, 1992

Cullen, Martin, ed., *Who's Who in Catholic Life*, Manchester: Gabriel Communications, 1997

Danson, John, ed., *The Catholic Directory*, Manchester: Gabriel Communications, 1999

Flannery, Austin, ed., *Vatican Council II*, Leominster: Fowler Wright Books Ltd, 1981 edition

Harrison, Ted, *Defender of the Faith*, London: Fount, 1996

Joyce, James, *The Dead*, London: Grant Richards, 1914

Keatinge, James, *The Priest – His character and his work*, London: Mackays, 1903

Kelly, Christine, ed., *The Enemy Within*, Milton Keynes: Family Publications, 1992

Lodge, David, *How Far Can You Go?*, London: Martin Secker & Warburg Ltd, 1980

Longford, Frank, *The Bishops*, London: Sidgwick & Jackson Ltd, 1986

Manning, Edward Henry, *The Eternal Priesthood*, London: Burns, Oates & Washbourne, 1880

Muggeridge, Malcolm, *Conversion*, London: Fount, 1988

Murphy-O'Connor, Cormac, *The Family of the Church*, London: Darton, Longman & Todd, 1983

Robinson, Josephine, *The Inner Goddess*, Leominster: Gracewing, 1998

Sharkey, Michael, ed., *Some Definite Service*, Manchester: Gabriel Communications, 1996

and

The many homilies, speeches and pastoral letters delivered by Cormac Murphy-O'Connor, 1977 to 2000.